Fodor's Pocket Acapulco

Second New Edition

GW00372442

Reprinted from *Fodor's Mexico*

Fodor's Travel Publications, Inc.
New York • Toronto • London • Sydney • Auckland
http://www.fodors.com/

Fodor's Pocket Acapulco

Editor: Edie Jarolim

Contributors: Robert Blake, Judy Blumenberg, Audra Epstein, Christina Knight, Wendy Luft, Erica Meltzer, M. T. Schwartzman, Craig Vetter

Creative Director: Fabrizio La Rocca

Associate Art Director: Guido Caroti

Photo Researcher: Jolie Novak

Cartographer: David Lindroth

Cover Photograph: Peter Guttman

Text Design: Between the Covers

Copyright

Second Edition

ISBN 0–679–03267–3

Special Sales

Fodor's Travel Publications are available at special discounts for sales promotions or premiums. Special editions, including personalized covers, excerpts of existing guides, and corporate imprints, can be created in large quantities for special needs. For more information, contact your local bookseller or write to Special Markets, Fodor's Travel Publications, 201 E. 50th St., New York, NY 10022; Random House of Canada, Ltd., Marketing Dept., 1265 Aerowood Dr., Mississaugua, Ontario L4W 1B9; Fodor's Travel Publications, 20 Vauxhall Bridge Rd., London SW1 2SA, England.

PRINTED IN THE UNITED STATES OF AMERICA

10 9 8 7 6 5 4 3 2 1

CONTENTS

Spanish Vocabulary   *100*

Index   *107*

Maps

ON THE ROAD WITH FODOR'S

WE'RE ALWAYS thrilled to get letters from readers, especially one like this:

It took us an hour to decide what book to buy and we now know we picked the best one. Your book was wonderful, easy to follow, very accurate, and good on pointing out eating places, informal as well as formal. When we saw other people using your book, we would look at each other and smile.

Our editors and writers are deeply committed to making every Fodor's guide "the best one"— not only accurate but always charming, brimming with sound recommendations and solid ideas, right on the mark in describing restaurants and hotels, and full of fascinating facts that make you view what you've traveled to see in a rich new light.

About Our Writers

When she was fresh out of college, our Acapulco and Pacific Coast Resorts correspondent **Wendy Luft** jumped at the chance to take a job with the Mexican tourist office—for a year or two at most, she figured. Some 25 years later, she and her Mexican husband and their adolescent sons, inveterate travelers all, traverse the country together from their home base in Mexico City. As a writer, editor, and public relations representative, Wendy has written and collaborated on many travel books and articles about her adopted country.

Editor **Edie Jarolim** first got a taste for Mexico in the late 1970s, when she attempted (unsuccessfully) to visit every Maya ruin in the Yucatán on a two-week vacation. Her frequent return forays have been made easier by a recent move to neighboring Arizona. She knows the Spanish conquistadors were a cruel bunch, but can't help but admire the good sense of a group who set out to vanquish Veracruz and Acapulco instead of, say, Saskatchewan.

New This Year

This year we've reformatted our guides to make them easier to use. **Destination: Acapulco** begins with brand-new recommended itineraries to help you decide what to see in the time you have. You may also notice our fresh graphics, new in 1996. More readable and more helpful than ever? We think so— and we hope you do, too.

We've rearranged the chapters a bit this year to make it easier for you to find the places you want to explore (*see* How to Use This Book, *below*). We also beefed up the shopping sections throughout, the better to help you indulge in one of Mexico's great pastimes.

Also check out Fodor's Web site (http://www.fodors.com/), where you'll find travel information on major destinations around the world and an ever-changing array of travel-savvy interactive features.

How to Use This Book

Organization

Up front is **Essential Information.** Its first section, **Important Contacts,** gives addresses and telephone numbers of organizations and companies that offer destination-related services and detailed information and publications. **Smart Travel Tips,** the second section, gives specific information on how to accomplish what you need to in Acapulco as well as tips on savvy traveling. Both sections are in alphabetical order by topic.

Icons and Symbols

★   Our special recommendations

✕   Restaurant

🏠   Lodging establishment

✕🏠   Lodging establishment whose restaurant warrants a detour

☞   Sends you to another section of the guide for more info

✉   Address

☎   Telephone number

FAX   Fax number

✆   Opening and closing times

🎟   Admission prices (those we give apply only to adults; substantially reduced fees are almost always available for children, students, and senior citizens)

Credit Cards

The following abbreviations are used: **AE,** American Express; **DC,** Diners Club; **MC,** MasterCard; and **V,** Visa.

Please Write to Us

You can use this book in the confidence that all prices and opening times are based on information supplied to us at press time; Fodor's cannot accept responsibility for any errors. Time inevitably brings changes, so always confirm information when it matters—especially if you're making a detour to visit a specific place. In addition, when making reservations be sure to mention if you have a disability or are traveling with children, if you prefer a private bath or a certain type of bed, or if you have specific dietary needs or any other concerns.

Were the restaurants we recommended as described? Did our

hotel picks exceed your expectations? Did you find a museum we recommended a waste of time? If you have complaints, we'll look into them and revise our entries when the facts warrant it. If you've discovered a special place that we haven't included, we'll pass the information along to our correspondents and have them check it out. So send your feedback, positive *and* negative, to the *Pocket Acapulco* Editor at Fodor's Travel Publications, 201 East 50th Street, New York, New York 10022—and have a wonderful trip!

Karen Cure
Editorial Director

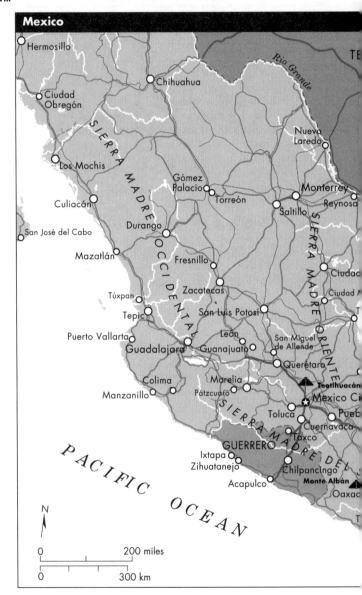

Mexico

Essential
Information

IMPORTANT CONTACTS

An Alphabetical Listing of Publications, Organizations, and Companies That Will Help You Before, During, and After Your Trip

AIR TRAVEL

The **Juan N. Alvarez International Airport** (☎ 011–52–748/40887) is about 20 minutes east of Acapulco.

CARRIERS

Aeromexico's (☎ 800/237–6639) flight from New York to Acapulco stops in Mexico City. The carrier also offers one-stop or connecting service from Atlanta, Chicago, Houston, Los Angeles, Miami, and Orlando. **American** (☎ 800/433–7300) has nonstop flights from Dallas, with connecting service from Chicago and New York. **American West** (☎ 800/235–9292) offers nonstop service from Phoenix. **Continental**'s (☎ 800/525–0280) direct flights are from Houston; **Delta**'s (☎ 800/241–4141) are from Los Angeles. **Mexicana** (☎ 800/531–7921) has nonstops from Chicago, and connecting service from Los Angeles, Miami, New York, San Antonio, and San Jose, California.

COMPLAINTS

To register complaints about charter and scheduled airlines, contact the U.S. Department of Transportation's **Aviation Consumer Protection Division** (⊠ C-75, Washington, DC 20590, ☎ 202/366–2220). Complaints about lost baggage or ticketing problems and safety concerns may also be logged with the **Federal Aviation Administration (FAA) Consumer Hotline** (☎ 800/322–7873).

CONSOLIDATORS

For the names of reputable air-ticket consolidators, contact the **United States Air Consolidators Association** (⊠ 925 L St., Suite 220, Sacramento, CA 95814, ☎ 916/441–4166, FAX 916/441–3520). For discount air-ticketing agencies, *see* Discounts & Deals, *below.*

CUTTING COSTS

For the lowest airfares to Acapulco, call 800/FLY-4–LESS or 800/FLY-ASAP.

BUS TRAVEL

ETN (☎ 5/273–0251) is a first-class bus line servicing Acapulco from Mexico City's Western Bus Terminal (*Terminal Central Poniente*).

CAR RENTAL

The major car-rental companies represented in Acapulco are **Avis** (☎ 800/331–1084; in Canada, 800/879–2847), **Budget** (☎ 800/527–0700; in the U.K., 0800/

181181), **Dollar** (☎ 800/800–4000; in the U.K., 0990/565656, where it is known as Eurodollar), **Hertz** (☎ 800/654–3001; in Canada, 800/263–0600; in the U.K., 0345/555888), and **National InterRent** (sometimes known as Europcar InterRent outside North America; ☎ 800/227–3876; in the U.K., 0345/222525).

Car-rental agencies at **Juan N. Alvarez International Airport** include **Avis** (☎ 74/62–00–85), **Hertz** (☎ 74/85–89–47), **Quick** (☎ 74/86–34–20), and **Saad** (☎ 74/84–34–45).

CAR INSURANCE
Experienced and reliable sources for Mexican car insurance are **Instant Mexico Auto Insurance** (✉ 223 Via de San Ysidro, San Ysidro, CA 92173, ☎ 619/428–3583) and **Sanborn's Mexican Insurance** (✉ 2009 S. 10th St., McAllen, TX 78505, ☎ 210/686–0711).

SERVICE
Mechanics in government-run, green pick-up trucks patrol major highways. *Los Angeles Verdes* (Green Angels) provide disabled vehicles free service except for parts and gas. Their 24-hour hot line is 250–82–21 or 250–85–55, ext. 314.

CRUISES
Many cruises include Acapulco as part of their itinerary. Most originate from Los Angeles. Cruise operators include **Crystal P & O** (☎ 212/972–4499), **Cunard Line** (☎ 800/5–CUNARD), **Holland America Lines** (☎ 800/628–4855), **Krystal Cruises** (☎ 800/446–6645), **Princess Cruises** (☎ 800/421–0522), **Regency Cruise Line** (☎ 213/785–9300), **Royal Caribbean Cruise Line** (☎ 800/327–6700), and **Royal Cruise Line** (☎ 800/227–4534). Bookings are generally handled through a travel agent.

CUSTOMS

U.S. CITIZENS
The **U.S. Customs Service** (✉ Box 7407, Washington, DC 20044, ☎ 202/927–6724) can answer questions on duty-free limits and publishes a helpful brochure, "Know Before You Go." For information on registering foreign-made articles, call 202/927–0540.

COMPLAINTS➤ Note the inspector's badge number and write to the commissioner's office (✉ 1301 Constitution Ave. NW, Washington, DC 20229).

CANADIANS
Contact **Revenue Canada** (✉ 2265 St. Laurent Blvd. S, Ottawa, Ontario K1G 4K3, ☎ 613/993–0534) for a copy of the free brochure "I Declare/Je Déclare" and for details on duty-free limits. For recorded information (within Canada only), call 800/461–9999.

U.K. CITIZENS
HM Customs and Excise (✉ Dorset House, Stamford St., London SE1 9NG, ☎ 0171/202–4227) can answer questions about U.K. cus-

toms regulations and publishes a free pamphlet, "A Guide for Travellers," detailing standard procedures and import rules.

DISABILITIES & ACCESSIBILITY

COMPLAINTS

To register complaints under the provisions of the Americans with Disabilities Act, contact the U.S. Department of Justice's **Disability Rights Section** (⊠ Box 66738, Washington, DC 20035, ☎ 202/514–0301 or 800/514–0301, FAX 202/307–1198, TTY 202/514–0383 or 800/514–0383). For airline-related problems, contact the U.S. Department of Transportation's **Aviation Consumer Protection Division** (☞ Air Travel, *above*).

ORGANIZATIONS

TRAVELERS WITH HEARING IMPAIRMENTS➤ The **American Academy of Otolaryngology** (⊠ 1 Prince St., Alexandria, VA 22314, ☎ 703/836–4444, FAX 703/683–5100, TTY 703/519–1585) publishes a brochure, "Travel Tips for Hearing Impaired People."

TRAVELERS WITH MOBILITY PROBLEMS➤ Contact the **Information Center for Individuals with Disabilities** (⊠ Box 256, Boston, MA 02117, ☎ 617/450–9888; in MA, 800/462–5015; TTY 617/424–6855); **Mobility International USA** (⊠ Box 10767, Eugene, OR 97440, ☎ and TTY 503/343–1284, FAX 503/343–6812), the U.S. branch of a Belgium-based organi-

zation (☞ *below*) with affiliates in 30 countries; **MossRehab Hospital Travel Information Service** (☎ 215/456–9600, TTY 215/456–9602), a telephone information resource for travelers with physical disabilities; the **Society for the Advancement of Travel for the Handicapped** (⊠ 347 5th Ave., Suite 610, New York, NY 10016, ☎ 212/447–7284, FAX 212/725–8253; membership \$45); and **Travelin' Talk** (⊠ Box 3534, Clarksville, TN 37043, ☎ 615/552–6670, FAX 615/552–1182), which provides local contacts worldwide for travelers with disabilities.

TRAVELERS WITH VISION IMPAIRMENTS➤ Contact the **American Council of the Blind** (⊠ 1155 15th St. NW, Suite 720, Washington, DC 20005, ☎ 202/467–5081, FAX 202/467–5085) for a list of travelers' resources.

IN THE U.K.

Contact the **Royal Association for Disability and Rehabilitation** (⊠ RADAR, 12 City Forum, 250 City Rd., London EC1V 8AF, ☎ 0171/250–3222) or **Mobility International** (⊠ rue de Manchester 25, B-1080 Brussels, Belgium, ☎ 00–322–410–6297, FAX 00–322–410–6874), an international travel-information clearinghouse for people with disabilities.

TRAVEL AGENCIES & TOUR OPERATORS

The Americans with Disabilities Act requires that all travel firms serve the needs of all travelers.

Agencies and operators specializing in making travel arrangements for individuals and groups with disabilities include **Access Adventures** (⌂ 206 Chestnut Ridge Rd., Rochester, NY 14624, ☎ 716/889–9096), run by a former physical-rehab counselor; and **CareVacations** (⌂ 5019 49th Ave., Suite 102, Leduc, Alberta T9E 6T5, ☎ 403/986–8332; in Canada, 800/648–1116), which has group tours and is especially helpful for cruises.

TRAVELERS WITH MOBILITY PROBLEMS➤ Contact **Accessible Journeys** (⌂ 35 W. Sellers Ave., Ridley Park, PA 19078, ☎ 610/521–0339 or 800/846–4537, FAX 610/521–6959), a registered nursing service that arranges vacations; **Hinsdale Travel Service** (⌂ 201 E. Ogden Ave., Suite 100, Hinsdale, IL 60521, ☎ 708/325–1335 or 800/303–5521), a travel agency that benefits from the advice of wheelchair traveler Janice Perkins; and **Wheelchair Journeys** (⌂ 16979 Redmond Way, Redmond, WA 98052, ☎ 206/885–2210 or 800/313–4751), which can handle arrangements worldwide.

DISCOUNTS & DEALS

CLUBS

Contact **Entertainment Travel Editions** (⌂ Box 1068, Trumbull, CT 06611, ☎ 800/445–4137; $28–$53, depending on destination), **Great American Traveler** (⌂ Box 27965, Salt Lake City, UT 84127, ☎ 800/548–2812; $49.95 per yr),

Moment's Notice Discount Travel Club (⌂ 7301 New Utrecht Ave., Brooklyn, NY 11204, ☎ 718/234–6295; $25 per yr, single or family), **Privilege Card International** (⌂ 3391 Peachtree Rd. NE, Suite 110, Atlanta, GA 30326, ☎ 404/262–0222 or 800/236–9732; $74.95 per yr), **Travelers Advantage** (⌂ CUC Travel Service, 49 Music Sq. W, Nashville, TN 37203, ☎ 800/548–1116 or 800/648–4037; $49 per yr, single or family), or **Worldwide Discount Travel Club** (⌂ 1674 Meridian Ave., Miami Beach, FL 33139, ☎ 305/534–2082; $50 per yr for family, $40 single).

GAY & LESBIAN TRAVEL

ORGANIZATIONS

The **International Gay Travel Association** (⌂ Box 4974, Key West, FL 33041, ☎ 800/448–8550, FAX 305/296–6633), a consortium of more than 1,000 travel companies, can supply names of gay-friendly travel agents, tour operators, and accommodations.

TOUR OPERATORS

Cruises and resort vacations for gays are handled by **R.S.V.P. Travel Productions** (⌂ 2800 University Ave. SE, Minneapolis, MN 55414, ☎ 612/379–4697 or 800/328–7787). **Olivia** (⌂ 4400 Market St., Oakland, CA 94608, ☎ 510/655–0364 or 800/631–6277) specializes in such bookings for lesbians. For mixed gay and lesbian travel, **Atlantis Events** (⌂ 9060

Santa Monica Blvd., Suite 310, West Hollywood, CA 90069, ☎ 310/281–5450 or 800/628–5268) and **Toto Tours** (⊠ 1326 W. Albion Ave., Suite 3W, Chicago, IL 60626, ☎ 312/274–8686 or 800/565–1241, ℻ 312/274–8695) offer group tours to worldwide destinations.

TRAVEL AGENCIES

The largest agencies serving gay travelers are **Advance Travel** (⊠ 10700 Northwest Fwy., Suite 160, Houston, TX 77092, ☎ 713/682–2002 or 800/292–0500), **Club Travel** (⊠ 8739 Santa Monica Blvd., West Hollywood, CA 90069, ☎ 310/358–2200 or 800/429–8747), **Islanders/Kennedy Travel** (⊠ 183 W. 10th St., New York, NY 10014, ☎ 212/242–3222 or 800/988–1181), **Now Voyager** (⊠ 4406 18th St., San Francisco, CA 94114, ☎ 415/626–1169 or 800/255–6951), and **Yellowbrick Road** (⊠ 1500 W. Balmoral Ave., Chicago, IL 60640, ☎ 312/561–1800 or 800/642–2488). **Skylink Women's Travel** (⊠ 2460 W. 3rd St., Suite 215, Santa Rosa, CA 95401, ☎ 707/570–0105 or 800/225–5759) serves lesbian travelers.

HEALTH ISSUES

FINDING A DOCTOR

For its members, the **International Association for Medical Assistance to Travellers** (⊠ IAMAT, membership free; 417 Center St., Lewiston, NY 14092, ☎ 716/754–4883; ⊠ 40 Regal Rd., Guelph, Ontario N1K 1B5, ☎ 519/836–0102; ⊠ 1287 St. Clair Ave. W, Toronto, Ontario M6E 1B8, ☎ 416/652–0137; ⊠ 57 Voirets, 1212 Grand-Lancy, Geneva, Switzerland, no phone) publishes a worldwide directory of English-speaking physicians meeting IAMAT standards.

MEDICAL ASSISTANCE COMPANIES

The following companies are concerned primarily with emergency medical assistance, although they may provide some insurance as part of their coverage. For a list of full-service travel insurance companies, *see* Insurance, *below.*

Contact **International SOS Assistance** (⊠ Box 11568, Philadelphia, PA 19116, ☎ 215/244–1500 or 800/523–8930; ⊠ Box 466, Pl. Bonaventure, Montréal, Québec H5A 1C1, ☎ 514/874–7674 or 800/363–0263; ⊠ 7 Old Lodge Pl., St. Margarets, Twickenham TW1 1RQ, England, ☎ 0181/744–0033), **Medex Assistance Corporation** (⊠ Box 5375, Timonium, MD 21094, ☎ 410/453–6300 or 800/537–2029), **Near Travel Services** (⊠ Box 1339, Calumet City, IL 60409, ☎ 708/868–6700 or 800/654–6700), **Traveler's Emergency Network** (⊠ 1133 15th St. NW, Suite 400, Washington, DC 20005, ☎ 202/828–5894 or 800/275–4836, ℻ 202/828–5896), **TravMed** (⊠ Box 5375, Timonium, MD 21094, ☎ 410/453–6380 or 800/732–5309), or **Worldwide Assistance Services**

(✉ 1133 15th St. NW, Suite 400, Washington, DC 20005, ☎ 202/331–1609 or 800/821–2828, ☏ 202/828–5896).

WARNINGS

The hot line of the **National Centers for Disease Control** (✉ CDC, National Center for Infectious Diseases, Division of Quarantine, Traveler's Health Section, 1600 Clifton Rd., M/S E-03, Atlanta, GA 30333, ☎ 404/332–4559, ☏ 404/332–4565) provides information on health risks abroad and vaccination requirements and recommendations. You can call for an automated menu of recorded information or use the fax-back service to request printed matter.

INSURANCE

IN THE U.S.

Travel insurance covering baggage, health, and trip cancellation or interruptions is available from **Access America** (✉ Box 90315, Richmond, VA 23286, ☎ 804/285–3300 or 800/284–8300), **Carefree Travel Insurance** (✉ Box 9366, 100 Garden City Plaza, Garden City, NY 11530, ☎ 516/294–0220 or 800/323–3149), **Near Travel Services** (✉ Box 1339, Calumet City, IL 60409, ☎ 708/868–6700 or 800/654–6700), **Tele-Trip** (✉ Mutual of Omaha Plaza, Box 31716, Omaha, NE 68131, ☎ 800/228–9792), **Travel Guard International** (✉ 1145 Clark St., Stevens Point, WI 54481, ☎ 715/345–0505 or 800/826–1300), **Travel Insured In-**

ternational (✉ Box 280568, East Hartford, CT 06128, ☎ 203/528–7663 or 800/243–3174), and **Wallach & Company** (✉ 107 W. Federal St., Box 480, Middleburg, VA 22117, ☎ 703/687–3166 or 800/237–6615).

IN CANADA

Contact **Mutual of Omaha** (✉ Travel Division, 500 University Ave., Toronto, Ontario M5G 1V8, ☎ 416/598–4321 or 800/268–8825).

IN THE U.K.

The **Association of British Insurers** (✉ 51 Gresham St., London EC2V 7HQ, ☎ 0171/600–3333) gives advice by phone and publishes the free pamphlet **"Holiday Insurance,"** which sets out typical policy provisions and costs.

MONEY MATTERS

CURRENCY EXCHANGE

If your bank doesn't exchange currency, contact **Thomas Cook Currency Services** (☎ 800/287–7362 for locations). **Ruesch International** (☎ 800/424–2923 for locations) can also provide you with foreign banknotes before you leave home and publishes a number of useful brochures, including a "Foreign Currency Guide" and "Foreign Exchange Tips." All major airports have 24-hour currency exchange booths.

WIRING FUNDS

Funds can be wired via **Money-Gram**[SM] (for locations and information in the U.S. and Canada, ☎ 800/926–9400) or **Western Union** (for agent locations or to send money using MasterCard or Visa, ☎ 800/325–6000; in Canada, 800/ 321–2923; in the U.K., 0800/ 833833; or visit the Western Union office at the nearest major post office).

PASSPORTS & VISAS

IN THE U.S.
For fees, documentation requirements, and other information, call the State Department's **Office of Passport Services** information line (☎ 202/647–0518).

CANADIANS
For fees, documentation requirements, and other information, call the Ministry of Foreign Affairs and International Trade's **Passport Office** (☎ 819/994–3500 or 800/ 567–6868).

U.K. CITIZENS
For fees, documentation requirements, and to request an emergency passport, call the **London Passport Office** (☎ 0990/210410).

SENIOR CITIZENS
Contact the **American Association of Retired Persons** (⌂ AARP, 601 E St. NW, Washington, DC 20049, ☎ 202/434–2277; annual dues $8 per person or couple). Its Purchase Privilege Program secures discounts for members on lodging, car rentals, and sightseeing.

Additional sources for discounts on lodgings, car rentals, and other travel expenses, as well as helpful magazines and newsletters, are the **National Council of Senior Citizens** (⌂ 1331 F St. NW, Washington, DC 20004, ☎ 202/347–8800; annual membership $12) and Sears's **Mature Outlook** (⌂ Box 10448, Des Moines, IA 50306, ☎ 800/336–6330; annual membership $9.95).

TELEPHONE MATTERS
The country code for Mexico is 52. To find out local Mexican access numbers from the United States, contact **AT&T** USADirect (☎ 800/874–4000), **MCI** Call USA (☎ 800/444–4444), or **Sprint** Express (☎ 800/793–1153). From within Mexico, **AT&T** USA Direct is accessed by dialing 95–800/462–4240 from any private or hotel phone, or any public phone marked "LADATEL." From the same phones, dial 95–800/674–7000 for **MCI** WorldPhone, or 95–800/877–8000 for **Sprint.**

TOUR OPERATORS
Among the companies that sell tours and packages to Acapulco, the following are nationally known, have a proven reputation, and offer plenty of options.

GROUP TOURS
Armadillo Tours International (⌂ 4301 Westbank Dr., Bldg. B360, Austin, TX 78746, ☎ 512/328–7800 or 800/284–5678), **Gadabout Tours** (for cruises) (⌂ 700 E. Tahquitz Canyon Way, Palm Springs, CA 92262, ☎ 619/325–

5556 or 800/952–5068), and **Go with Jo** (⊠ 910 Dixieland Rd., Harlingen, TX 78552, ☎ 210/423–1446 or 800/999–1446, FAX 210/421–5787).

PACKAGES

For independent vacation packages, contact **American Airlines Fly AAway Vacations** (☎ 800/321–2121) and **Delta Dream Vacations** (☎ 800/872–7786). **Funjet Vacations,** based in Milwaukee, Wisconsin, and **Gogo Tours,** based in Ramsey, New Jersey, sell packages only through travel agents.

Regional operators often feature nonstop flights for travelers from their local area. Arrangements may include charter or scheduled air. Contact **Apple Vacations** (⊠ 25 N.W. Point Blvd., Elk Grove Village, IL 60007, ☎ 708/640–1150 or 800/365–2775), **Friendly Holidays** (⊠ 1983 Marcus Ave., Lake Success, NY 11042, ☎ 800/344–5687), and **Travel Impressions** (⊠ 465 Smith St., Farmingdale, NY 11735, ☎ 516/845–8000 or 800/284–0044, FAX 516/845–8095).

FROM THE U.K.

Bales Tours (⊠ Bales House, Junction Rd., Dorking, Surrey RH4 3HB, ☎ 01306/876–881 or 01306/885–991, FAX 01306/740–048), **British Airways Holidays** (⊠ Astral Towers, Betts Way, London Rd., Crawley, West Sussex RH10 2XA, ☎ 01293/723–121, FAX 01293/722–624),

Journey Latin America (⊠ 14–16 Devonshire Rd., Chiswick, London W4 2HD, ☎ 0181/747–8315, FAX 0181/742–1312), and **Kuoni Travel** (⊠ Kuoni House, Dorking, Surrey RH5 4AZ, ☎ 01306/742–222, FAX 01306/744–222).

For a custom-designed holiday contact **Steamond Travel** (⊠ 23 Eccleston St., London SW1 9LX, ☎ 0171/286–4449, FAX 0171/730–3024) or **Trailfinders** (⊠ 42–50 Earls Court Rd., London W8 6FT, ☎ 0171/937–5400, FAX 0171/938–3305).

THEME TRIPS

FISHING➤ **Aeromexico Vacations** (☎ 800/245–8585), the airline's in-house tour program, offers comprehensive packages including air, hotel, and sportfishing. For more boat charters and vacation packages contact **Anglers Travel** (⊠ 3100 Mill St., No. 206, Reno, NV 89502, ☎ 702/324–0580 or 800/624–8429, FAX 702/324–0583), **Cutting Loose Expeditions** (⊠ Box 447, Winter Park, FL 32790-0447, ☎ 407/629–4700 or 800/533–4746), **Fishing International** (⊠ Box 2132, Santa Rosa, CA 95405, ☎ 800/950–4242), **Mexico Sportsman** (⊠ 202 Milam Bldg., San Antonio, TX 78205, ☎ 210/212–4566 or 800/633–3085, FAX 210/212–4568), and **Rod and Reel Adventures** (⊠ 3507 Tully Rd., No. B6, Modesto, CA 95356-1052, ☎ 209/524–7775 or 800/356–6982, FAX 209/524–1220).

For bookings and information about sportfishing in the Ixtapa/Zihuatanejo area, contact **Ixtapa Sportfishing Charters** (⊠ 33 Olde Mill Run, Stroudsburg, PA 18360, ☎ 717/424–8323, FAX 717/424–1016; in Zihuatanejo, ☎ 755/4–44–26 or 755/4–41–62).

GOLF➣ **Stine's Golftrips** (⊠ Box 2314, Winter Haven, FL 33883-2314, ☎ 941/324–1300 or 800/428–1940, FAX 941/325–0384, golftrip@cris.com) sells resort-based golf packages that include confirmed tee times and golfing fees and lessons.

ORGANIZATIONS

The **National Tour Association** (⊠ NTA, 546 E. Main St., Lexington, KY 40508, ☎ 606/226–4444 or 800/755–8687) and the **United States Tour Operators Association** (⊠ USTOA, 211 E. 51st St., Suite 12B, New York, NY 10022, ☎ 212/750–7371) can provide lists of members and information on booking tours.

TRAIN TRAVEL

There is no train service to Acapulco from anywhere in the United States or Canada, nor is there service from Mexico City.

TRAVEL AGENCIES

For names of reputable agencies in your area, contact the **American Society of Travel Agents** (⊠ ASTA, 1101 King St., Suite 200, Alexandria, VA 22314, ☎ 703/739–2782), the **Association of British Travel Agents** (⊠ 55-57 Newman St., London W1P 4AH, ☎ 0171/637–2444, FAX 0171/637–0713), or the **Association of Canadian Travel Agents** (⊠ Suite 201, 1729 Bank St., Ottawa, Ontario K1V 7Z5, ☎ 613/521–0474, FAX 613/521–0805).

IN ACAPULCO

American Express (⊠ La Gran Plaza shopping center, Costera Miguel Alemán 1628, locals 7, 8, and 9, ☎ 74/69–11–00 to 09); **Viajes Wagon-Lits** (⊠ Westin Las Brisas Hotel, Scenic Hwy. 5255, ☎ 74/84–16–50, ext. 392).

VISITOR INFORMATION

Mexico Ministry of Tourism Web site: http://mexico-travel.com/. To receive information on Acapulco by fax, dial FAX 541/385–9282, and enter the numbers 2, 2271, your fax number, and 2272 through 2275 at the appropriate prompts.

State of Guerrero Department of Tourism (SEFOTUR) (⊠ Costera Miguel Alemán 187, across from Bodegas Aurrerá, ☎ 74/86–91–64 or 74/86–91–71. ☉ Mon.–Sat. 9–2 and 4–7).

WEATHER

For current conditions and forecasts, plus the local time and helpful travel tips, call the **Weather Channel Connection** (☎ 900/932–8437; 95¢ per min) from a Touch-Tone phone.

SMART TRAVEL TIPS

Basic Information on Traveling in Acapulco and Savvy Tips to Make Your Trip a Breeze

ADDRESSES

The Mexican method of naming streets is exasperatingly arbitrary, so **be patient when searching for street addresses.** Many Mexican addresses have "s/n" for *sin número* (no number) after the street name. This is common in small towns where there are fewer buildings on a block. Similarly, many hotels give their address as "Km 30 a Querétaro," which indicates that the property is on the main highway 30 kilometers (19 miles) from Querétaro.

As in Europe, addresses in Mexico are written with the street name first, followed by the street number. The five-digit zip code (*código postal*) precedes, rather than follows, the name of the city. "Apdo." (*apartado*) means "post office box number."

Veteran travelers to Mexico invariably make one observation about asking directions in the country: Rather than say that they do not know, some Mexicans will offer well-intended guidance that may or may not be correct. Instead of asking "Is the so-and-so this way?" (which often elicits a smiling affirmative, regardless of the truth of the matter), try "Where is the so-and-so?"

AIR TRAVEL

If time is an issue, **always look for nonstop flights,** which require no change of plane. If possible, **avoid connecting flights,** which stop at least once and can involve a change of plane, even though the flight number remains the same; if the first leg is late, the second waits.

From New York via Dallas, flying time is 4½ hours; from Chicago, 4¼ hours; from Los Angeles, 3½ hours.

AIRPORT TRANSFERS

Private taxis are not permitted to carry passengers from the airport to town, so most people rely on **Transportes Aeropuerto** (☎ 73/66–99–88), a special airport taxi service. The system looks confusing, but there are dozens of helpful English-speaking staff to help you figure out which taxi to take.

Look for the name of your hotel and the number of its zone on the overhead sign on the walkway in front of the terminal. Then go to the desk designated with that zone number and buy a ticket for an airport taxi. The ride from the airport to the hotel zone on the trip costs about $3.50 per person for the *colectivo* and starts at $17 for a nonshared cab, depending on your destination. The drivers are usually helpful and will often take you to hotels that aren't on their list. Tips are optional. The journey into town takes 20 to 30 minutes.

CUTTING COSTS

The Sunday travel section of most newspapers is a good place to look for deals.

MAJOR AIRLINES➤ The least-expensive airfares from the major airlines are priced for round-trip travel and are subject to restrictions. Usually, you must **book in advance and buy the ticket within 24 hours** to get cheaper fares, and you may have to **stay over a Saturday night.** The lowest fare is subject to availability, and only a small percentage of the plane's total seats is sold at that price. It's smart to **call a number of airlines, and when you are quoted a good price, book it on the spot—** the same fare may not be available on the same flight the next day. Airlines generally allow you to change your return date for a $25 to $50 fee. If you don't use your ticket, you can apply the cost toward the purchase of a new ticket, again for a small charge. However, most low-fare tickets are nonrefundable. To get the lowest airfare, **check different routings.** If your destination has more than one gateway, **compare prices to different airports.**

FROM THE U.K.➤ To save money on flights, **look into an APEX or Super-Pex ticket.** APEX tickets must be booked in advance and have certain restrictions. Super-PEX tickets can be purchased right at the airport.

CONSOLIDATORS➤ Consolidators buy tickets for scheduled flights at reduced rates from the airlines, then sell them at prices below the lowest available from the airlines directly—usually without advance restrictions. Sometimes you can even get your money back if you need to return the ticket. Carefully read the fine print detailing penalties for changes and cancellations. If you doubt the reliability of a consolidator, **confirm your reservation with the airline.**

CHARTER FLIGHTS➤ Charters usually have the lowest fares and most restrictions. Departures are infrequent and seldom on time, and you can lose all or most of your money if you cancel. (The closer to departure you cancel, the more you lose, although sometimes you can pay only a small fee if you supply a substitute passenger.) The flight may be canceled for any reason up to 10 days before departure (after that, only if it is physically impossible to operate). The charterer may also revise the itinerary or increase the price after you have bought the ticket, but only if the new arrangement constitutes a "major change" do you have the right to a refund. Before buying a charter ticket, **read** the fine print regarding the company's refund policies. Money for charter flights is usually paid into a bank escrow account, the name of which should be on the contract, and if you don't pay by credit card, make your check payable to the carrier's escrow account (unless you're dealing with a travel agent, in which case his or her check should be made payable to the escrow account). The U.S. Department of Transportation's Aviation Consumer Protection Division has jurisdiction over charters.

Charter operators may offer flights alone or with ground arrangements that constitute a charter package. Normally, you must book charters through a travel agent.

BUS TRAVEL

TO ACAPULCO
Bus service from Mexico City to Acapulco is excellent. First-class buses, which leave every hour on the hour from the Tasqueña station, are comfortable and in good condition. The trip takes 5½ hours, and a one-way ticket costs about $13. There is also deluxe service, called *Servicio Diamante*, with airplanelike reclining seats, refreshments, rest rooms, air-conditioning, movies, and hostess service. The deluxe buses leave four times a day, also from the Tasqueña station, and cost about $21. *Futura* service (regular reclining seats, air-conditioning, and a rest room) costs $15.

IN ACAPULCO
The buses tourists use the most are those that go from Puerto Marqués to Caleta and stop at the fairly conspicuous metal bus stops along the way. If you want to go from the zócalo to the Costera, catch the bus that says "La Base" (the naval base near the Hyatt Regency). This bus detours through Old Acapulco and returns to the Costera just east of the Ritz Hotel. If you want to follow the Costera for the entire route, take the bus marked "Hornos." Buses to Pie de la Cuesta or Puerto Marqués say so on the front. The Puerto Marqués bus runs about every half hour and is always crowded. If you are headed anywhere along the Costera Miguel Alemán, it's best to go by the Aca Tur bus. For 30¢ you can ride in deluxe, air-conditioned vehicles that travel up and down the main drag from the Hyatt to the Caleta hotels every 10 minutes.

BUSINESS HOURS

BANKS
Banks are generally open weekdays 9 AM to 1:30 PM. In some larger cities, a few also open weekdays 4 to 6 PM, Saturday 10 AM to 1:30 PM and 4 to 6 PM, and Sunday 10 AM to 1:30 PM; however, the extended hours are often for deposits only. Banks will give you cash advances in pesos (for a fee) if you have a major credit card.

GOVERNMENT OFFICES

Government offices are usually open 8 AM to 3 PM; along with banks and most private offices, they are closed on national holidays.

STORES

Hours are generally weekdays and Saturday from 9 or 10 AM to 7 or 8 PM; in resort areas, shops may also be open on Sunday. Business hours are 9 AM to 7 PM, with a two-hour lunch break (siesta) from about 2 to 4 PM.

CAR RENTAL

The trip to Acapulco from Mexico City on the old road takes about six hours. A privately built and run four-lane toll road connecting Mexico City with Acapulco is expensive (about $28 one-way) but well maintained, and it cuts driving time between the two cities from six hours to 3½ hours. Many people opt for going via Taxco, which can be reached from either road.

When considering this option, consider that you may be sharing the road with some less-than-ideal drivers (sometimes acquiring a driver's license in Mexico is more a question of paying someone off than of having tested skill). In addition, the highway system is very uneven: In some regions, modern, well-paved superhighways prevail; in others, particularly the mountains, potholes, untethered live-stock, and dangerous, unrailed curves are the rule.

If you plan to visit some of the more remote beaches or decide to visit Taxco on your own, renting a car is convenient but fairly expensive. Prices start at about $50 a day for a Volkswagen sedan without air-conditioning. Don't expect a full tank; your car will have just about enough gas to get you to the nearest Pemex station.

CUTTING COSTS

To get the best deal, **book through a travel agent who is willing to shop around.** Ask your agent to **look for fly-drive packages,** which also save you money, and **ask if local taxes are included** in the rental or fly-drive price. These can be as high as 20% in some destinations. Don't forget to find out about required deposits, cancellation penalties, drop-off charges, and the cost of any required insurance coverage.

Also **ask your travel agent about a company's customer-service record.** How has it responded to late plane arrivals and vehicle mishaps? Are there often lines at the rental counter, and—if you're traveling during a holiday period—does a confirmed reservation guarantee you a car?

Always **find out what equipment is standard** at your destination before specifying what you want; automatic transmission and air-conditioning are usually optional—and very expensive.

INSURANCE

When driving a rented car, you are generally responsible for any damage to or loss of the rental vehicle, as well as any property damage or personal injury that you cause. Before you rent, **see what coverage you already have** under the terms of your personal auto insurance policy and credit cards.

If you do not have auto insurance or an umbrella insurance policy that covers damage to third parties, purchasing CDW or LDW is highly recommended.

When you drive in Mexico, it is necessary at all times to **carry proof of Mexican auto liability insurance,** which is usually provided by car-rental agencies and included in the cost of the rental. If you don't have proof of insurance and happen to injure someone—whether it's your fault or not—you stand the risk of being jailed.

LICENSE REQUIREMENTS

In Mexico your own driver's license is acceptable. An International Driver's Permit is a good idea; it's available from the American or Canadian automobile associations, or, in the United Kingdom, from the AA or RAC.

SURCHARGES

There is a 10% tax on all car rentals. Before you pick up a car in one city and leave it in another, **ask about drop-off charges or one-way service fees,** which can be substantial. Note, too, that

some rental agencies charge extra if you return the car before the time specified on your contract. To avoid a hefty refueling fee, **fill the tank just before you turn in the car** (3.78 liters = 1 gallon)—but be aware that gas stations near the rental outlet may overcharge. There is no self-service at stations.

CHILDREN & TRAVEL

All children, including infants, must have proof of citizenship for travel to Mexico. Children traveling with a single parent must also have a notarized letter from the other parent stating that the child has his or her permission to leave their home country. In addition, parents must now fill out a tourist card for each child traveling with them.

BABY-SITTING

For recommended local sitters, **check with your hotel desk.**

LODGING

Most hotels allow children under a certain age to stay in their parents' room at no extra charge; others charge them as extra adults. Be sure to **ask about the cutoff age.**

CONSULATES

United States (⊠ Club del Sol Hotel, ☎ 74/85–72–07); **Canada** (⊠ Club del Sol Hotel, ☎ 74/85–66–21).

CUSTOMS & DUTIES

To speed your clearance through customs, **keep receipts for all your**

purchases abroad and **be ready to show the inspector what you've bought.** If you feel that you've been incorrectly or unfairly charged a duty, you can **appeal assessments in dispute.** First ask to see a supervisor. If you are still unsatisfied, **write to the port director** at your point of entry, sending your customs receipt and any other appropriate documentation. The address will be listed on your receipt. If you still don't get satisfaction, you can take your case to customs headquarters in Washington.

Upon entering Mexico, you will be given a baggage declaration form and asked to itemize what you're bringing into the country. You are allowed to bring in 2 liters of spirits or wine for personal use; 400 cigarettes, 50 cigars, or 250 grams of tobacco; a reasonable amount of perfume for personal use; one movie camera and one regular camera and 12 rolls of film for each; and gift items not to exceed a total of $300. You are not allowed to bring meat, vegetables, plants, fruit, or flowers into the country.

IN THE U.S.
You may bring home $400 worth of foreign goods duty-free if you've been out of the country for at least 48 hours and haven't already used the $400 allowance, or any part of it, in the past 30 days.

Travelers 21 or older may bring back 1 liter of alcohol duty-free, provided the beverage laws of the state through which they reenter the United States allow it. Regardless of the traveler's age, they are allowed 100 non-Cuban cigars and 200 cigarettes. Antiques and works of art more than 100 years old are duty-free.

Duty-free, travelers may mail packages valued at up to $200 to themselves and up to $100 to others, with a limit of one parcel per addressee per day (and no alcohol or tobacco products or perfume valued at more than $5); on the outside, the package should be labeled as being either for personal use or an unsolicited gift, and a list of its contents and their retail value should be attached. Mailed items do not affect your duty-free allowance on your return.

IN CANADA
If you've been out of Canada for at least seven days, you may bring in C$500 worth of goods duty-free. If you've been away for fewer than seven days but for more than 48 hours, the duty-free allowance drops to C$200; if your trip lasts between 24 and 48 hours, the allowance is C$50. You cannot pool allowances with family members. Goods claimed under the C$500 exemption may follow you by mail; those claimed under the lesser exemptions must accompany you.

Alcohol and tobacco products may be included in the seven-day and 48-hour exemptions but not in the 24-hour exemption. If you meet the age requirements of the province or territory through which you reenter Canada, you may bring in, duty-free, 1.14 liters (40 imperial ounces) of wine or liquor *or* 24 12-ounce cans or bottles of beer or ale. If you are 16 or older, you may bring in, duty-free, 200 cigarettes, 50 cigars or cigarillos, and 400 tobacco sticks or 400 grams of manufactured tobacco. Alcohol and tobacco must accompany you on your return.

An unlimited number of gifts with a value of up to C$60 each may be mailed to Canada duty-free. These do not affect your duty-free allowance on your return. Label the package "Unsolicited Gift—Value Under $60." Alcohol and tobacco are excluded.

IN THE U.K.

From countries outside the EU, including Mexico, you may import, duty-free, 200 cigarettes, 100 cigarillos, 50 cigars, or 250 grams of tobacco; 1 liter of spirits or 2 liters of fortified or sparkling wine or liqueurs; 2 liters of still table wine; 60 milliliters of perfume; 250 milliliters of toilet water; plus £136 worth of other goods, including gifts and souvenirs.

DINING

Mexican restaurants run the gamut from humble hole-in-the-wall shacks, street stands, *taquerías*, and American-style fast-food joints to internationally acclaimed gourmet restaurants. Prices, naturally, follow suit. To save money, **look for the fixed-menu lunch known as co-mida corrida** or menú del día, which is served between 1 and 4 PM almost everywhere in Mexico.

Lunch is the big meal; dinner is rarely served before 8 PM. There is no government rating of restaurants, but you'll know which ones cater to tourists simply by looking at the clientele and the menu (bilingual menus usually mean slightly higher prices than at non-tourist restaurants). Credit cards—especially MasterCard and Visa—are increasingly accepted.

DISCOUNTS & DEALS

You may already be eligible for all kinds of savings. Here are some time-honored strategies for getting the best deal.

LOOK IN YOUR WALLET

When you **use your credit card to make travel purchases,** you may get free travel-accident insurance, collision damage insurance, medical or legal assistance, depending on the card and bank that issued it. American Express, Visa, and MasterCard provide one or more of these services, so **get a copy of your card's travel benefits.** If you are a member of the AAA or an oil-company-sponsored road-assistance plan, always **ask hotel or car-rental reservationists for auto-club discounts.** Some clubs offer additional discounts on tours, cruises, or admission to attractions. And don't forget that auto-club membership entitles you to free maps and trip-planning services.

SENIORS CITIZENS & STUDENTS

As a senior-citizen traveler, you may be eligible for special rates, but you should mention your senior-citizen status up front.

DIAL FOR DOLLARS

To save money, **look into "1-800" discount reservations services,** which often have lower rates. These services use their buying power to get a better price on hotels, airline tickets, and sometimes even car rentals. When booking a room, always **call the hotel's local toll-free number** (if one is available) rather than the central reservations number—you'll often get a better price. Ask the reservationist about special packages or corporate rates, which are usually available even if you're not traveling on business.

JOIN A CLUB?

Discount clubs can be a legitimate source of savings, but you must use the participating hotels and visit the participating attractions in order to realize any benefits. Remember, too, that you have to pay a fee to join, so **determine if you'll save enough to warrant your membership fee.** Before booking with a club, **make sure the hotel or other supplier isn't offering a better deal.**

GET A GUARANTEE

When shopping for the best deal on hotels and car rentals, **look for guaranteed exchange rates,** which protect you against a falling dollar. With your rate locked in, you won't pay more even if the price goes up in the local currency.

DOCTORS & DENTISTS

Your hotel can locate an English-speaking doctor, but they don't come cheap—house calls are about $100. The U.S. consular representative has a list of doctors and dentists, but it's against their policy to recommend anyone in particular.

EMERGENCIES

Police (☎ 74/85–06–50). **Red Cross** (☎ 74/85–41–22). Two reliable hospitals are **Hospital Privado Magallanes** (✉ Wilfrido Massiue 2, ☎ 74/85–65–44) and **Hospital Centro Médico** (✉ J. Arevalo 620, ☎ 74/82–46–92).

ENGLISH-LANGUAGE BOOKSTORES

English-language books and periodicals can be found at **Sanborns,** a reputable American-style department-store chain, and at the newsstands in some of the larger hotels. Many small newsstands and the Super-Super carry the *Mexico City News* and the *Mexico City Times,* English-language daily newspapers that are flown in from Mexico City. *Acapulco Heat,* also in English, is a good source of information about local events and gossip.

GAY & LESBIAN TRAVEL

Same-sex couples keep a low profile in Mexico, and two people of the same gender can often have a hard time getting a *cama matrimonial* (double bed), especially in smaller hotels. However, alternative lifestyles (whether they be homosexuality or any other bending of conventional roles) are more easily accepted in metropolitan centers such as Acapulco.

GUIDED TOURS

ORIENTATION TOURS

There are organized tours everywhere in Acapulco, from the red-light district to the lagoon. Tours to Mexican fiestas in the evenings or the markets in the daytime are easy to arrange. Tour operators have offices around town and desks in many of the large hotels. If your hotel can't arrange a tour, contact **Consejeros de Viajes** at the Torre de Acapulco (⊠ Costera Miguel Alemán 1252, ☎ 74/84–74–00) or **Turismo Caleta** (⊠ Andrea Doria 2, in Costa Azul, ☎ 74/84–65–70).

SUNSET CRUISES

The famous cliff divers at La Quebrada (☞ Chapter 2) give one performance in the afternoon and four performances every night. For about $27, **Divers de México** organizes sunset champagne cruises that provide a fantastic view of the spectacle from the water. For reservations, call 74/82–13–98 or stop by the office downtown near the *Fiesta* and *Bonanza* yachts. The *Fiesta* (☎ 74/83–18–03) runs cruises at 7:30 PM on Tuesday, Thursday, and Saturday for about $24. The *Bonanza*'s (☎ 74/83–18–03) sunset cruise, with open bar (domestic drinks) and live and disco music, costs about $10. All boats leave from downtown near the zócalo (town square). Many hotels and shops sell tickets, as do the ticket sellers on the waterfront.

HEALTH CONCERNS

SHOTS AND MEDICATIONS

According to the Centers for Disease Control and Prevention (CDC), there is a limited risk of malaria and dengue fever in certain rural areas of Mexico. Travelers in most urban or easily accessible areas need not worry. However, if you plan to visit remote regions or stay for more than six weeks, **check with the CDC's International Travelers Hotline** (☞ Important Contacts, *above*). In areas with malaria and dengue, which are both carried by mosquitoes, take mosquito nets, wear clothing that covers the body, apply repellent containing DEET, and use a spray against flying insects in living and sleeping areas. The hot line recommends chloroquine (analen) as an anti-malarial agent; no vaccine exists against dengue.

The major health risk in Mexico is posed by the contamination of drinking water, fresh fruit, and vegetables by fecal matter, which causes the intestinal ailment known as traveler's diarrhea. To prevent it, **watch what you eat and drink.** Stay away from uncooked food and unpasteurized milk and milk products, and **drink only bottled water or water that has been boiled** for at least 20 minutes. When ordering cold drinks at untouristed establishments, skip the ice: *sin hielo.* (You can usually identify ice made commercially from purified water by its uniform shape and the hole in the center.) Hotels with water purification systems will post signs to that effect in the rooms. *Tacos al pastor*—thin pork slices grilled on a spit and garnished—are delicious but dangerous. Be wary of Mexican hamburgers, because you can never be certain what meat they are made with (horsemeat is very common).

If these measures fail, try paregoric, a good antidiarrheal agent that dulls or eliminates abdominal cramps, which requires a doctor's prescription in Mexico; or in mild cases, Pepto-Bismol or Imodium (loperamide), which can be purchased over the counter. Get plenty of purified water or tea—chamomile is a good folk remedy for diarrhea. In severe cases, rehydrate yourself with a salt-sugar solution (½ teaspoon salt and 4 tablespoons sugar per quart/liter of water).

SUNBURN

Caution is advised when venturing out in the Mexican sun. Sunbathers lulled by a slightly overcast sky or the sea breezes can be burned badly in just 20 minutes. To avoid overexposure, **use strong sunscreens and avoid the peak sun hours** of noon to 2 PM.

DIVERS' ALERT

Scuba divers take note: **Do not fly within 24 hours of scuba diving.**

INSURANCE

Travel insurance can protect your monetary investment, replace your luggage and its contents, or provide for medical coverage should you fall ill during your trip. Most tour operators, travel agents, and insurance agents sell specialized health-and-accident, flight, trip-cancellation, and luggage insurance as well as comprehensive policies with some or all of these coverages. Comprehensive policies may also reimburse you for delays due to weather—an important consideration if you're traveling during the winter months. Some health-insurance policies do not cover preexisting conditions, but waivers may be available in specific cases. Coverage is sold by the companies listed in Important Contacts; these companies act as the policy's administrators. The actual insurance is usually underwritten by a well-known name, such as the Travelers or Continental Insurance.

Before you make any purchase, **review your existing health and home-owner's policies** to find out whether they cover expenses incurred while traveling.

BAGGAGE

Airline liability for baggage is limited to $1,250 per person on domestic flights. On international flights, it amounts to $9.07 per pound or $20 per kilogram for checked baggage (roughly $640 per 70-pound bag) and $400 per passenger for unchecked baggage. Insurance for losses exceeding the terms of your airline ticket can be bought directly from the airline at check-in for about $10 per $1,000 of coverage; note that it excludes a rather extensive list of items, shown on your airline ticket.

COMPREHENSIVE

Comprehensive insurance policies include all the coverages described above plus some that may not be available in more specific policies. If you have purchased an expensive vacation, especially one that involves travel abroad, comprehensive insurance is a must; **look for policies that include trip delay insurance,** which will protect you in the event that weather problems cause you to miss your flight, tour, or cruise. A few insurers will also sell you a waiver for preexisting medical conditions. Some of the companies that offer both these features are Access America, Carefree Travel, Travel Insured

International, and TravelGuard (☞ Important Contacts, *above*).

FLIGHT

You should **think twice before buying flight insurance.** Often purchased as a last-minute impulse at the airport, it pays a lump sum when a plane crashes, either to a beneficiary if the insured dies or sometimes to a surviving passenger who loses his or her eyesight or a limb. Supplementing the airlines' coverage described in the limits-of-liability paragraphs on your ticket, it's expensive and basically unnecessary. Charging an airline ticket to a major credit card often automatically provides you with coverage that may also extend to travel by bus, train, and ship.

HEALTH

Medicare generally does not cover health-care costs outside the United States; nor do many privately issued policies. If your own health insurance policy does not cover you outside the United States, **consider buying supplemental medical coverage.** It can reimburse you for $1,000–$150,000 worth of medical and/or dental expenses incurred as a result of an accident or illness during a trip. These policies also may include a personal-accident, or death-and-dismemberment, provision, which pays a lump sum ranging from $15,000 to $500,000 to your beneficiaries if you die or to you if you lose one or more limbs or your eyesight, and a medical-assistance provision, which may either reimburse you for the cost of referrals, evacuation, or repatriation and other services, or automatically enroll you as a member of a particular medical-assistance company. (☞ Health Issues *in* Important Contacts, *above.*)

TRIP

Without insurance, you will lose all or most of your money if you cancel your trip regardless of the reason. Especially if your airline ticket, cruise, or package tour is nonrefundable and cannot be changed, it's essential that you **buy trip-cancellation-and-interruption insurance.** When considering how much coverage you need, look for a policy that will cover the cost of your trip plus the nondiscounted price of a one-way airline ticket should you need to return home early. Read the fine print carefully, especially sections that define "family member" and "preexisting medical conditions." Also **consider default or bankruptcy insurance,** which protects you against a supplier's failure to deliver. Be aware, however, that if you buy such a policy from a travel agency, tour operator, airline, or cruise line, it may not cover default by the firm in question.

U.K. TRAVELERS

You can buy an annual travel insurance policy valid for most vacations during the year in which it's purchased. If you are pregnant or have a preexisting medical condition, make sure you're covered before buying such a policy.

LANGUAGE

Spanish is the official language of Mexico and basic English is widely understood by most people employed in tourism.

As in most other foreign countries, knowing the mother tongue has a way of opening doors, so **learn some Spanish words and phrases.** Mexicans are not scornful of visitors' mispronunciations and grammatical errors; on the contrary, they welcome even the most halting attempts to use their language. For a rudimentary vocabulary, featuring many terms travelers are likely to encounter in Mexico, *see* the Spanish Vocabulary section at the end of this guide.

LODGING

Hotel rates are subject to the 10% value-added tax, and service charges and meals are generally not included. The Mexican government categorizes hotels, based on qualitative evaluations, into *gran turismo* (superdeluxe hotels, of which there are only about 50 nationwide); five-star down to one-star; and economy class. Keep in mind that many hotels that might otherwise be rated higher have opted for a lower category to avoid higher interest rates on loans and financing.

Mexican hotels—particularly those owned or managed by the international chains—are always being expanded. In older properties, travelers may often have to choose between newer annexes with modern amenities and rooms in the original buildings with possibly fewer amenities and—equally possible, but not certain—greater charm.

MONEY & EXPENSES

As of January 1, 1993, the new unit of currency in Mexico became the *nuevo peso*, or new peso, which is subdivided into 100 centavos. At press time, the peso was still recovering from the devaluation enacted by the Zedillo administration. While exchange rates were as favorable as one U.S. dollar to NP$6.02, one Canadian dollar to NP$4.4, and a pound sterling to 9.7, the market and prices are likely to have adjusted themselves by 1997.

The old peso, which had a cumbersome exchange of 3,000 to one U.S. dollar, was to be completely phased out by January 1994, but at press time there was still old currency in circulation, and many public phones and vending machines in rural areas still accepted only the old coins. The new paper currency differs in design and, in some cases, size, from the old and comes in denominations of 10, 20, 50, 100, 200, and 500. The new 10-, 20-, 50-, and 100-peso bills are equal to the old 10,000, 20,000, 50,000 and 100,000 notes, respectively. Newly introduced were the 2-, 5-, 10-, and 20-peso coins. The 1,000-, 500-, 200-, 100-, and 50-peso coins were replaced by the smaller, newly designed 1-peso and 50-, 20-, 10-, and 5-centavo coins. Needless to say, it is somewhat confusing. Travelers should **examine coins carefully before paying and when receiving change.** Note: NP$ generally precedes prices in new pesos. To avoid fraud, it's wise to make sure that "NP" is clearly marked on all credit-card receipts.

Traveler's checks and all major U.S. credit cards (except Discover) are accepted in most tourist areas of Mexico. The large hotels, restaurants, and department stores accept cards readily. Some of the smaller restaurants and shops, however, will only take cash. When shopping, you can usually get much better prices if you **bargain with dollars.**

ATMS

CASH ADVANCES➤ Before leaving home, **make sure that your credit cards have been programmed for ATM use in Acapulco.** Note that Discover is accepted mostly in the United States. Local bank cards often do not work overseas either; **ask your bank about a Visa debit card,** which works like a bank card but can be used at any ATM displaying a Visa logo.

TRANSACTION FEES➤ Although fees charged for ATM transactions may be higher abroad than at home, Cirrus and Plus exchange rates are excellent, because they are based on wholesale rates offered only by major banks.

COSTS

Acapulco is one of the most expensive places to visit in Mexico. Although the peso devalued in late 1995, prices of the large chain hotels, calculated in dollars, have not gone down, and some restaurant owners and merchants have raised their prices to compensate for the devaluation.

EXCHANGING CURRENCY

For the most favorable rates, **change money at banks.** You won't do as well at exchange booths in airports or rail and bus stations, in hotels, in restaurants, or in stores, although you may find their hours more convenient. To avoid lines at airport exchange booths, **get a small amount of the local currency before you leave home.**

TAXES

AIRPORT➤ An airport departure tax of U.S. $12 or the peso equivalent must be paid at the airport for international flights from Mexico, and there is a domestic air departure tax of around U.S. $6. Traveler's checks and credit cards are not accepted.

VAT➤ Mexico has a value-added tax of 10% called I.V.A. (*impuesto de valor agregado*), which is occasionally (and illegally)

waived for cash purchases. Other taxes and charges apply for phone calls, dining, and lodging.

TRAVELER'S CHECKS

The most widely recognized checks are issued by American Express, Citicorp, Thomas Cook, and Visa. These are sold by major commercial banks for 1%–3% of the checks' face value—it pays to **shop around.** So you won't be left with excess foreign currency, **buy a few checks in small denominations** to cash toward the end of your trip.

PACKING FOR ACAPULCO

Pack light: Though baggage carts are available now at airports, luggage restrictions on international flights are tight, and you'll want to save space for purchases. Mexico is filled with bargains on textiles, leather goods, arts and crafts, and silver jewelry.

Mexico operates on the 110-volt system, which is the same as in the United States and Canada.

Resorts are both casual and elegant; you'll see high-style designer sportswear, tie-dyed T-shirts, cotton slacks and walking shorts, and plenty of colorful sundresses. The sun can be fierce; **bring a sun hat (or buy one locally) and sunscreen for the beach and for sightseeing.** You'll need a sweater or jacket to cope with hotel and restaurant air-conditioning, which can be glacial. Few restaurants require a jacket and tie.

PASSPORTS & VISAS

If you don't already have one, **get a passport.** It is advisable that you **leave one photocopy of your passport's data page** with someone at home and keep another with you, separated from your passport, while traveling. If you lose your passport, promptly call the nearest embassy or consulate and the local police; having the data page information can speed replacement.

IN THE U.S.

For short stays, any proof of citizenship is sufficient for entry into Mexico. Minors also need parental permission. All U.S. citizens, even infants, need a valid passport or a certified birth certificate, notarized affadavit of citizenship, or voter's registration card, plus a photo I.D. to enter Mexico for stays of more than 180 days. Application forms for both first-time and renewal passports are available at any of the 13 U.S. Passport Agency offices and at some post offices and courthouses. Passports are usually mailed within four weeks; allow five weeks or more in spring and summer.

CANADIANS

You need only a valid passport to enter Mexico for stays of up to six months. Passport application forms are available at 28 regional passport offices, as well as post offices and travel agencies. Whether for a first or a renewal passport, you must apply in person. Children under 16 may be included on a parent's passport but must have their own to travel alone. Passports are valid for five years and are usually mailed within two to three weeks of application.

U.K. CITIZENS

Citizens of the United Kingdom need only a valid passport to enter Mexico for stays of up to three months. Applications for new and renewal passports are available from main post offices and at the passport offices in Belfast, Glasgow, Liverpool, London, Newport, and Peterborough. You may apply in person at all passport offices, or by mail to all except the London office. Children under 16 may travel on an accompanying parent's passport. All passports are valid for 10 years. Allow a month for processing.

PERSONAL SECURITY & COMFORT

Just as you would anywhere, **use common sense.** Wear a money belt; put valuables in hotel safes; avoid driving on untraveled streets and roads at night; and carry your own baggage whenever possible. Reporting a crime to the police is often a frustrating experience unless you speak excellent Spanish and have a great deal of patience.

Women traveling alone are likely to be subjected to *piropos* (cat-calls). To avoid this, try not to wear tight clothes or enter street bars or cantinas alone. Your best strategy is always to try and ignore the offender and go on about your business. If the situation seems to be getting out of hand, do not hesitate to ask someone for help. *Piropos* are one thing, but outright harassment of women is not considered acceptable behavior. If you express outrage, you should find no shortage of willing defenders.

SHOPPING

At least three varieties of outlets sell Mexican crafts: indoor and outdoor municipal markets, shops run by Fonart (a government agency to promote Mexican crafts), and tourist boutiques in towns, shopping malls, and hotels. If you **buy in the municipal shops or markets** you can avoid the VAT, and you'll be able to pay in pesos or dollars. You'll have to have patience and a good eye here: Bargains are to be had, but quality may be inconsistent. Fonart shops are a good reference for quality and price (the latter are fixed). Boutiques usually accept credit cards if not dollars; although they are overpriced, they are also convenient. (You may be asked to pay up to 10% more on credit card purchases; savvy shoppers with cash have greater bargaining clout.) The 10% tax (I.V.A.) is charged on most purchases but is often disregarded by eager or desperate vendors.

Bargaining is widely accepted in the markets, but you should understand that not all vendors will start out with outrageous prices. If you feel the price quoted is too high, start off by offering no more than half the asking price and then slowly go up, usually to about 70% of the original price. Always shop around.

If you buy woolens or wood items, it's wise to freeze or microwave them when you return to destroy possible insect infestation. Keep in mind that buying items made from tortoiseshell and black coral contributes to ecological destruction. Furthermore, such items are not allowed into the United States.

TAXIS

Taxis are available on the street, at taxi stands (*sitios*), and by phone.

Government-certified taxis have a license with a photo of the driver and a taxi number prominently displayed, as well as a meter. More often than not, however, the meter is "broken." In this case, agree upon a price before setting off. Tipping is not necessary unless the driver helps you with your bags, in which case a few pesos are appropriate.

How much you pay depends on what type of taxi you get. The most expensive are hotel taxis. A price list that all drivers adhere to is posted in hotel lobbies. Fares in town are usually about $1.50 to $3; to go from downtown to the Princess Hotel or Caleta Beach is about $6 to $12. Hotel taxis are by far the plushest and are kept in the best condition. In all cases, if you are unsure of what a fare should be, ask your hotel's front desk personnel or bell captain.

Cabs that cruise with their roof light off occasionally carry a price list but usually charge by zone. There is a minimum charge of $1.50; the fare should still be less than it would be at a hotel. Some taxis that cruise have hotel or restaurant names stenciled on the side but are not affiliated with an establishment.

The cheapest taxis are the little Volkswagens. Officially there is a $1.50 minimum charge, but some cab drivers don't stick to it. A normal—i.e., Mexican-priced—fare is about $1.50 to go from the zócalo to the International Center. Rates are about 50% higher at night, and though tipping is not expected, Mexicans usually leave small change.

You can also hire a taxi by the hour or the day. Prices vary from about $12 an hour for a hotel taxi to $8 an hour for a street taxi. Never let a taxi driver decide where you should eat or shop, since many get kickbacks from some of the smaller stores and restaurants.

AT THE AIRPORT

From the airport, **take a government-subsidized cab**; the driver will accept the taxi vouchers sold at stands inside or just outside the airport, which in theory ensure that

your fare is established beforehand. However, in practice you may be overcharged, so prepare yourself by locating the taxi originating and destination zones on a map and make sure your ticket is properly zoned; if you only need a ticket from zone three to zone four, don't pay for a ticket from zone one.

The rates for non-government-subsidized cabs routinely exceed the official taxi rate. For distances more than several kilometers, negotiate a rate in advance; many drivers will start by asking how much you want to pay to get a sense of how street-smart you are.

TELEPHONES

The variety of public phones that exist in the country can be confusing; **use the traditional black, square phones with push buttons or dials to make local calls for free.** Newer phones have both a coin slot and one or more unmarked slots for credit cards or LADATEL telephone calling cards; **look for LADATEL phones to make long-distance calls.** LADATEL (the Spanish acronym for "long-distance direct dialing") cards can be purchased at tourist offices as well as at newsstands and stores with a LADATEL logo. They come in denominations of up to NP$50. Some Mexican phones may accept U.S. Visa or MasterCard. U.S. calling cards can be used from LADATEL phones only with the appropriate access code (☞ Telephone Matters *in* Important Contacts, *above*).

So far, there is still no Touch-Tone (digital) circuitry in operation in Mexico. Although some hotel, office, and residence phones have a "tone/pulse" switch, if you think you'll need to access an automated phone system or voice mail in the United States, it's a good idea to **take along a Touch-Tone simulator** (you can buy them for about $17 at most electronic stores). Many phone numbers are in the process of being changed; a recording may offer the new number, so it's useful to learn the Spanish words for numbers 1 through 9 (☞ Spanish Vocabulary Section in the back of this book).

LONG-DISTANCE

The long-distance services of AT&T, MCI, and Sprint make calling home relatively convenient, but in many hotels you may find it impossible to dial the access number. The hotel operator may also refuse to make the connection. Instead, the hotel will charge you a premium rate—as much as 400% more than a calling card—for calls placed from your hotel room. To avoid such price gouging, travel with more than one company's long-distance calling card—a hotel may block Sprint but not MCI. If the hotel operator claims that you cannot use any phone card, ask to be connected to an international operator, who will help you to access your phone card. You can also dial the international operator yourself. If none of this works,

try calling your phone company collect in the United States. If collect calls are also blocked, call from a pay phone in the hotel lobby. Before you go, **find out the local access codes** for your destinations (☞ Telephone Matters *in* Important Contacts, *above*).

TIPPING

When tipping in Mexico, remember that the minimum wage is the equivalent of $6 a day and that the vast majority of workers in the tourist industry live barely above the poverty line. However, there are Mexicans who think in dollars and know, for example, that in the United States porters are tipped about $1 a bag; many of them expect the peso equivalent from foreigners but are happy to accept NP$1 from Mexicans. They will complain either verbally or with a facial expression if they feel they deserve more—you and your conscience must decide. Following are some general guidelines, in pesos.

Gas station attendants: 50 centavos.

Maids: NP$3 per night (all hotels).

Parking attendants and theater ushers: NP$2–NP$3; some theaters have set rates.

Porters at expensive hotels: NP$7 per bag.

Porters and bellboys at airports and at moderate and inexpensive hotels: NP$4 per bag.

Taxi drivers: Tipping necessary only if the driver helps with your bags—NP$3–NP$7 should be sufficient, depending on the extent of the help.

Waiters: 10%–15% of the bill, depending on service (make sure a 10%–15% service charge has not already been added to the bill, although this practice is not common in Mexico).

TOUR OPERATORS

A package or tour to Mexico can make your vacation less expensive and more hassle-free. Firms that sell tours and packages reserve airline seats, hotel rooms, and rental cars in bulk and pass some of the savings on to you. In addition, the best operators have local representatives available to help you at your destination.

BIG VS. SMALL➤ Operators that handle several hundred thousand travelers per year can use their purchasing power to give you a good price. Their high volume may also indicate financial stability. But some small companies provide more personalized service; because they tend to specialize, they may also be more knowledgeable about a given area.

A GOOD DEAL?

The more your package or tour includes, the better you can predict the ultimate cost of your vacation. Make sure you know exactly what is covered, and **beware of hidden costs.** Are taxes, tips, and service charges included? Transfers and baggage handling? Entertainment and excursions? These can add up.

Most packages and tours are rated deluxe, first-class superior, first class, tourist, or budget. The key difference is usually accommodations. If the package or tour you are considering is priced lower than in your wildest dreams, **be skeptical.** Also, **make sure your travel agent knows the accommodations** and other services. Ask about the hotel's location, room size, beds, and whether it has a pool, room service, or programs for children, if you care about these. Has your agent been there in person or sent others you can contact?

BUYER BEWARE

Each year a number of consumers are stranded or lose their money when operators—even very large ones with excellent reputations—go out of business. To avoid becoming one of them, take the time to **check out the operator**—find out how long the company has been in business and ask several agents about its reputation. Next, **don't book unless the firm has a consumer-protection program.** Members of the USTOA and the NTA are required to set aside funds for the sole purpose of covering your payments and travel arrangements in case of default. Nonmember operators may instead carry insurance; look for the details in the operator's brochure—and for the name of an underwriter with a solid reputation. Note: When it comes to tour operators, **don't trust escrow accounts.** Although there are laws governing those of charter-flight operators, no governmental body prevents tour operators from raiding the till.

Next, **contact your local Better Business Bureau and the attorney general's offices** in both your own state and the operator's; have any complaints been filed? Finally, **pay with a major credit card.** Then you can cancel payment, provided that you can document your complaint. Always **consider trip-cancellation insurance** (☞ Insurance, *above*).

SINGLE TRAVELERS

Prices are usually quoted per person, based on two sharing a room. If traveling solo, you may be required to pay the full double-occupancy rate. Some operators eliminate this surcharge if you agree to be matched up with a roommate of the same sex, even if one is not found by departure time.

TRAVEL AGENTS

Travel agents are excellent resources. In fact, large operators accept bookings made only through travel agents. But it's good to **collect brochures from several agencies** because some agents' suggestions may be skewed by promotional relationships with tour and package firms that reward them for volume sales.

WHEN TO GO

The weather in Acapulco is basically the same all year, with an average temperature of 80°F or 27°C. The hottest months are June, July, and August; the coolest is January. During the high season, December 15 to Easter, it rarely rains. The summer is more humid, August and October being the rainiest months. Whatever the time of year, the water is always warm. Low season (July to October) offers the advantage of lower prices and fewer people, though some restaurants and hotels close for vacation or to make repairs.

November is considered a "shoulder" month; prices will be midway between those in effect in high and low seasons. But even in low season, tour operators fill up the biggest hotels. The peak time for crowds is December 25 to January 3, when you may have trouble booking a hotel room. *Semana Santa,* the week before Easter, is very popular with Mexicans; schools are in recess and families come to Acapulco for their children's vacation. Budget hotels get very noisy and many tourists party all night and sleep on the beaches. Remember, no matter when you want to visit, book ahead to avoid disappointment.

The average daily maximum and minimum temperatures for Acapulco are as follows:

Climate in Acapulco

Jan.	88F	31C	May	90F	32C	Sept.	90F	32C
	72	22		77	25		77	25
Feb.	88F	31C	June	90F	32C	Oct.	90F	32C
	72	22		77	25		77	25
Mar.	88F	31C	July	91F	33C	Nov.	90F	32C
	72	22		77	25		75	24
Apr.	88F	31C	Aug.	91F	33C	Dec.	88F	31C
	72	22		77	25		73	23

1 Destination: Acapulco

SPLASHING INTO ACAPULCO

FOR SUN LOVERS, beach bums, and other hedonists, Acapulco is the ideal holiday resort. Don't expect high culture, historic monuments, or haute cuisine. Anyone who ventures to this Pacific resort 433 kilometers (260 miles) south of Mexico City does so to relax. Translate that as swimming, shopping, and enjoying the nightlife. Everything takes place against a staggeringly beautiful natural backdrop. Acapulco Bay is one of the world's best natural harbors, and it is the city's centerpiece. By day the water looks temptingly deep blue; at night it flashes and sparkles with the city lights.

The weather is Acapulco's major draw—warm waters, almost constant sunshine, and year-round temperatures in the 80s. It comes as no surprise, then, that most people plan their day around laying their towel on some part of Acapulco's many miles of beach. Both tame and wild water sports are available—everything from waterskiing to snorkeling, diving, and parasailing. Less strenuous possibilities are motorboat rides and fishing trips. Championship golf courses, tennis courts, and the food and crafts markets also occasionally lure some visitors away from the beach, but not out of the sun.

Most people rouse themselves from their hammocks, deck chairs, or towels only when it is feeding time. Eating is one of Acapulco's great pleasures. In addition to the glitzy places, there are many good no-frills, down-home Mexican restaurants. Eating at one of these spots gives you a glimpse into the real Mexico: office workers breaking for lunch, groups of men socializing over a cup of coffee.

At night Acapulco is transformed as the city rouses itself from the day's torpor and prepares for the long hours ahead. Even though Acapulco's heyday is past, its nightlife is legendary. This is true despite the fact that many of the discos along the main drag still look as if they were designed in the early '70s by an architect who bought mirrors and strobe lights wholesale. Perpetually crowded, the discos are grouped in twos and threes, so most people go to several places in one night.

Acapulco was originally an important port for the Spanish, who used it to trade with countries in the Far East. The Spanish built

Fuerte de San Diego (Fort San Diego) to protect the city from pirates, and today the fort houses a historical museum. The name of the late Teddy Stauffer, an entrepreneurial Swiss, is practically synonymous with that of modern Acapulco. He hired the first cliff divers at La Quebrada in Old Acapulco and founded the Boom Boom Room, the town's first dance hall, and Tequila A Go-Go, its first discotheque. The Hotel Mirador at La Quebrada and the area stretching from Caleta to Hornos beaches, near today's Old Acapulco, were the center of activity in the 1950s, when Acapulco was a town of 20,000 with an economy based largely on fishing.

Former president Miguel Alemán Valdés bought up miles of the coast just before the road and the airport were built. Avenida Costera Miguel Alemán bears his name today. Since the late 1940s, Acapulco has expanded eastward so that today it is one of Mexico's largest cities, with a population of approximately 2 million. Currently under development is a 3,000-acre expanse known as Acapulco Diamante, which encompasses the areas known as Punta Diamante and Playa Diamante and some of Acapulco's glitziest hotels and residential developments.

— Anya Schiffrin
Updated by Wendy Luft

PLEASURES AND PASTIMES

Beaches
The lure of sun and sand in Acapulco is legendary. Every sport is available, and you can eat in a beach restaurant, dance, and sleep in a *hamaca* (hammock) without leaving the water's edge. If you want to avoid the crowds, there are also plenty of quiet and even isolated beaches within reach.

Dining
Dining in Acapulco is more than just eating out—it is the most popular leisure activity in town. Every night the restaurants fill up, and every night the adventurous diner can sample a different cuisine: Italian, Belgian, Japanese, American, Tex-Mex, and, of course, plain old Mex. The variety of styles matches the range of cuisines: from greasy spoons that serve regional specialties to gourmet restaurants with gorgeous views of Acapulco Bay. Most restaurants fall somewhere in the middle, and on the Costera are dozens of beachside restaurants, roofed with palapa (palm frond), as well as wildly decorated rib and hamburger joints popular with visitors under 30—not necessarily in age, but definitely in spirit.

Another plus for Acapulco dining is that the food is garden fresh. Each morning the Mercado Municipal is abuzz with restaurant managers and locals buying up the fish, poultry, and vegetables that will appear on plates that evening. Although some top-quality beef is now being produced in the states of Sonora and Chihuahua, many of the more expensive restaurants claim that they import their beef from the States. Whether or not they're telling the truth, the beef is excellent in most places. Establishments that cater to tourists purify their drinking water and use it to cook vegetables.

Lodging

Accommodations in Acapulco run the gamut from sprawling, big-name complexes with nonstop amenities to small, family-run inns where hot water is a luxury. Wherever you stay, however, prices will be reasonable compared with those in the United States, and service is generally good, since Acapulqueños have been catering to tourists for more than 40 years.

Nightlife

Acapulco has always been famous for its nightlife, and justifiably so. For many visitors the discos and restaurants are just as important as the sun and the sand. The minute the sun slips over the horizon, the Costera comes alive with people milling around window-shopping, deciding where to dine, and generally biding their time till the disco hour. The legendary Acapulco discos are open 365 days a year from about 10:30 PM until they empty out, often not until 4 or 5 AM. Obviously you aren't going to find great culture here; theater efforts are few and far between and there is no classical music. But disco-hopping is a high art in Acapulco, and for those who care to watch, there are live shows and folk-dance performances.

Shopping

The abundance of air-conditioned shopping malls and boutiques makes picking up gifts and souvenirs one of the highlights of a visit to Acapulco. The malls are filled with clothing shops, and many others are strung along the Costera. There are also a few high-fashion boutiques that carry custom-designed clothes. Malls in Acapulco range from the shopping arcades at several of the more lavish hotels to the huge completely enclosed and air-conditioned Plaza Bahía.

The Mercado Municipal, whose rows are piled high with fruits, vegetables, poultry, fish, and meats, is also is a good source of local handicrafts. Flea markets abound, carrying what seems to be an inexhaustible supply of inexpensive collectibles and souvenirs.

Silver is a real bargain in Mexico. Taxco, three hours away, is one of the silver capitals of the world.

Sports and the Outdoors

Acapulco has lots for sports lovers to enjoy. Most hotels have pools, and many have several private tennis clubs as well as courts. The fitness craze has caught on, and many of the hotels have gyms, too. Acapulco's waters are teeming with sailfish, marlin, shark, and mahimahi, and although the waters aren't as clear as in the Caribbean, scuba diving is popular, as are waterskiing, windsurfing, kayaking, and bronco riding (an activity done in one-person motorboats). Parasailing is an Acapulco highlight. It looks terrifying and can be dangerous, but most people who do it love the view and go back again and again. Golfers can tee off at the nine-hole municipal course, in town, or at one of the five 18-hole championship courses (three are open to the public) in the Acapulco Diamante area.

GREAT ITINERARIES

It's possible to get a feel for Acapulco during a short stay if you take in some downtown sights along with your beach activities. Those who have a longer time to spend can really soak up the ambience of the place and can enjoy excursions to some isolated beaches as well as to Taxco.

If You Have 3 Days

Spend the first day enjoying your favorite beach activity, be it parasailing, waterskiing, or simply sunning. That evening, to get the lay of the land, take a sunset cruise that includes a ringside view of Acapulco's daredevil *clavadistas* (divers) at **La Quebrada.** The following day, experience Acapulco at its most authentic, paying an early visit to the **Mercado Municipal,** the **waterfront,** and the **zocálo** (town square). After some late afternoon shopping in the boutiques and handicrafts markets along the Costera Miguel Alemán, "shake off the dust" (as they say in Mexico) at one of the city's glitzy discos. The next day you'll want to try to land a sailfish, take in the Mexican Fiesta at the **Acapulco International Center** (drinks and show only), and bid farewell to Acapulco with a late candlelit dinner at one of the city's romantic dining spots.

If You Have 5 Days

Add on to the three-day itinerary a visit to **El Fuerte de San Diego,** built in the 18th century to protect Acapulco from pirates, and today home of the Anthropology Museum. For a taste of the 1950s Acapulco of John Wayne and Johnny Weissmuller, get a taxi to take you up in the hills above Caleta and Caletilla. Head out to Pie de la Cuesta for a late lunch and boat ride or waterskiing on Coyuca Lagoon, and then cross the road and park your body under a palm-frond umbrella for a spectacular sunset on the beach. Especially if you're traveling with kids, devote a day to **Mágico Mundo Marino** and the glass-bottom boat trip to Roqueta Island.

If You Have 7 Days

For a complete change of pace, you'll want to rent a car or arrange for a tour to **Taxco,** a glorious treasure of twisting cobblestone streets and some 1,000 silver shops, about a three-hour drive from Acapulco; plan to spend the night. For a change from shopping for silver, visit the Santa Prisca church, Taxco's most important landmark, on Plaza Borda, and the Casa Humboldt, which now houses a museum of viceregal art. Try to get a front-row seat at one of the bars or restaurants on the square and spend about an hour watching the constant activity: weddings, communions, funerals and baptisms, and vendors selling baskets and painted animals. The following day, before the return trip to Acapulco, tour the **Caves of Cacahuamilpa,** an amazing expanse of subterranean chambers.

2 Exploring Acapulco

ACAPULCO is a city that is easily understood, easily explored. During the day the focus for most visitors is the beach and the myriad activities that happen on and off it. At night the attention shifts to the restaurants and discos. The Costera Miguel Alemán, the wide boulevard that hugs Acapulco Bay from the Scenic Highway to Caleta Beach (about 8 kilometers, or 5 miles), is central to both day and night diversions. All the major beaches, shopping malls, and big hotels—minus the more exclusive Acapulco Diamante properties—are off the Costera. Hence most of the shopping, dining, and clubbing takes place within a few blocks of this main drag, and many an address is listed only as "Costera Miguel Alemán." Although the Costera runs completely across Acapulco, most of the action is between the naval base, La Base, next to the Hyatt (which anchors the eastern terminus of the Costera) and Papagayo Park. Because street addresses are not often used and streets have no logical pattern, directions are usually given from a major landmark, such as CiCi (a theme park) or the zócalo.

Old Acapulco, the colonial part of town and the only area of Acapulco that can easily be visited on foot, is where the Mexicans go to run their errands: mail letters at the post office, buy supplies at the Mercado Municipal, and pay their taxes. Also known as El Centro, it's where you'll find the zócalo, the church, and Fort San Diego. Just up the hill from Old Acapulco is La Quebrada.

The peninsula south of Old Acapulco contains remnants of the first version of Acapulco. This primarily residential area was prey to dilapidation and abandonment for many years, but efforts were made to revitalize it—such as re-opening the Caleta Hotel and opening the aquarium on Caleta Beach and the zoo on Roqueta Island. Although its prime is definitely past, it is now a popular area for budget travelers, especially Mexican and European. The Plaza de Toros, where bullfights are held on Sundays from Christmas to Easter, is in the center of the peninsula.

If you arrived by plane, you've already had a royal intro-
duction to Acapulco Bay. Acapulco Diamante is the area
stretching east of Acapulco proper from Las Brisas to Barra
Vieja beach. You'll need a car or a taxi to explore this area,
where you'll find most of Acapulco's poshest hotels—
Westin Las Brisas, the Acapulco Sheraton, Camino Real,
the Princess and Pierre Marqués, and Vidafel—and residential developments, as well as several exclusive private
clubs, pounding surf, and beautiful beaches.

A Good Tour

*Numbers in the text correspond to numbers in the margin
and on the Exploring Acapulco map.*

If you want to get the lay of the land, you might take a
drive or taxi ride along the Costera Miguel Alemán, start-
ing on its eastern edge at **La Base,** the Mexican naval base
south of Playa Icacos. When you come to Playa Icacos,
you'll see the **Casa de la Cultura** ① cultural complex on
the beach side (just past the Hyatt Regency hotel); a little farther down is **CiCi** ②, a children's amusement park.
About a kilometer (half mile) past CiCi, on the right side
of the Costera, lies the **Acapulco International Center**
(often called the Convention Center); you might return
here in the evening to attend a Mexican fiesta. Continue
along through the commercial heart of the Costera until
you reach **Papagayo Park** ③, one of the top municipal
parks in the country. When you arrive at the intersection
of the Costera with Pro. D. H. de Mendoza, detour a few
blocks inland to find Old Acapulco and the sprawling **Mercado Municipal** ④. You'll want to park your car nearby
or have your taxi drop you off; it's best to navigate this
area by foot. A few blocks west and closer to the water,
El Fuerte de San Diego ⑤ sits on the hill overlooking the
harbor next to the army barracks. You'll next see the
waterfront ⑥ (locally known as the *malecón*) with its series of docks and, adjoining it, the **zócalo** ⑦, the center
of Old Acapulco. A 15-minute walk up the hill from the
zócalo brings you to **La Quebrada** ⑧, where the famous
cliff divers do their daredevil stunt daily.

Sights to See

❶ Casa de la Cultura. This cultural complex includes a small archaeological museum, an exhibit of crafts from the entire state of Guerrero, and the Ixcateopan art gallery, with changing exhibits. ⊠ *Costera Miguel Alemán 4834,* ☎ *74/84–38–14.* ☐ *Free.* ☉ *Weekdays 9–2 and 5–8, Sat. 9–2.*

❷ CiCi (Centro Internacional para Convivencia Infantil). A water-oriented theme park for children, CiCi features dolphin and seal shows, a freshwater pool with wave-making apparatus, a water slide, miniaquarium, and other attractions. ⊠ *Costera Miguel Alemán, across from the Hard Rock Cafe,* ☎ *74/84–82–10.* ☐ *$5.* ☉ *Daily 10–6.*

❺ El Fuerte de San Diego. An 18th-century fortress, El Fuerte de San Diego was designed to protect the city from pirates. (The original fort, destroyed in an earthquake, was built in 1616.) The fort now houses the **Museo Historico de Acapulco,** under the auspices of Mexico's National Institute of Anthropology and History. The exhibits portray the city from prehistoric times through Mexico's independence from Spain in 1821. Especially noteworthy are the displays touching on the Christian missionaries sent from Mexico to the Far East and the cultural interchange that resulted. ⊠ *Calle Hornitos and Morelos,* ☎ *74/ 82–38–28.* ☐ *$2; free Sun.* ☉ *Tues.–Sun. 10:30–4:40.*

❽ La Quebrada. High on a hill above downtown Acapulco, La Quebrada is home to the Mirador Hotel, *the* place for tourists in the 1940s; it still retains some sheen from its glory days. But these days most visitors eventually make the trip here because this is where the famous cliff divers jump from a height of 130 feet daily at 1 PM and evenings at 7:30, 8:30, 9:30, and 10:30. The dives are thrilling, so be sure to arrive early. Before they take the plunge, the brave divers say a prayer at a small shrine near the jumping-off point. Sometimes they dive in pairs; often they carry torches. There's an admission fee (about $1), paid at a booth outside the hotel before you enter the viewing area; when you exit, some of the divers may also be waiting to greet you—and to ask for tips. (For information about viewing the divers on sunset cruises, *see* Guided Tours *in* Smart Travel Tips.)

🐚 ❾ **Mágico Mundo Marino.** In addition to an aquarium, the Magic Marine World features a sea lion show, swimming pools, a toboggan, scuba diving, and (for rent) Jet Skis, inner tubes, bananas (inflatable rubber tubes pulled along the beach by motorboats), and kayaks—not to mention clean rest rooms. From Mágico Mundo Marino, you can take the glass-bottom boat to **Roqueta Island** (about 10 minutes each way) for a visit to the small zoo. Palao's restaurant on Roqueta Island has a sandy cove for swimming, a pony, and a cage of monkeys that entertain youngsters. ⊠ *Caleta Beach, no phone.* ⊡ *Aquarium $3; round-trip ferry service to Roqueta Island, including zoo, $2.50.* ☉ *Mágico Mundo daily 9–7; zoo daily 9–5.*

❹ **Mercado Municipal.** It's not for everyone, but the sprawling municipal market is Acapulco as the locals experience it. They come to purchase their everyday needs, from fresh vegetables and candles to plastic buckets and love potions. The stalls within the mercado are densely packed together but are awning-covered, so things stay relatively cool despite the lack of air-conditioning.

There are hundreds of souvenirs to choose from here: woven blankets, puppets, colorful wooden toys and plates, leather goods, baskets, hammocks, and handmade wooden furniture, including child-size chairs. There is even a stand offering charms, amulets and talismans, bones, herbs, fish eyes, sharks' teeth, lotions, candles, and soaps said to help one find or keep a mate, increase virility or fertility, bring peace to the home, or ward off the evil eye. Kitschy gems abound: Acapulco ashtrays and boxes covered with tiny shells or enormous framed pictures of the Virgin of Guadalupe. There are also silver jewelry vendors, but unless you really have a good eye for quality, it's best to buy silver only from a reputable dealer (☞ Chapter 8).

It's best to come as early as possible to avoid the crowds. Ask to be dropped off near the *flores* (flower stand) closest to the souvenir and crafts section; from the flower stall, as you face the ceramic stand, turn right and head into the market. If you've driven to the mercado, locals may volunteer to watch your car; be sure to lock your trunk and tip about 35¢. ⊠ *Viaducto Aguas Blancas and Constituyentes, a few blocks west of the Costera.*

12

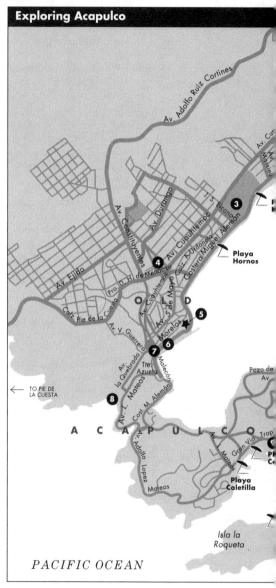

Exploring Acapulco

Av. Adolfo Ruiz Cortines

Av. Constituyentes

Av. Durango

J. S. Elcanon

Av. Cuauhtémoc

Calz. B. Urdaneta

Costera Miguel Alemán

Playa Hornos

Av. Ejido

Pro. D. H. de Mendoza

Calz. Pie de la Cuesta

O L D

Av. Cuauhtémoc

Av. S. Maceo López

Morelos

5

6

7

Av. la Quebrada

Av. V. Guerrero

Tte. Azueta

Malecón

← TO PIE DE LA CUESTA

8

Av. L. Mateos

Costa M. Alemán

A C A P U L C O

Av. Adolfo Lopez

Av. Matala

Gran Vía Trop

Pozo de

Av.

Mateos

Playa Caletilla

Isla la Roqueta

PACIFIC OCEAN

Av. Rancho
Acapulco

Paseo del Farallón

**Acapulco
International
Center**

Golf
Course

Lobo Solitario

Av. Almirante J. Morales

Av. Cuauhtémoc

Av. Massieu

Diana
Glorieta

Costera Miguel Alemán

Av. Cristóbal Colón

Av. Heroico Colegio

Magallanes

Av. Nelson

Costera Miguel Alemán

**Playa
Condesa**

**Playa
Icacos**

2 **1**

**Playa
Hornitos**

*Bahía de
Acapulco*

*Punta
Guitarrón*

Carretera Escénica

A C A P U L C O

D I A M A N T E

del Rey
Av.

Tropical

9

**Playa
Caleta**

TO AIRPORT →

*Bahía de
Puerto
Marqués*

Punta Bruja

**Playa
Roqueta**

TO PUNTA DIAMANTE →
AND BARRA VIEJA

N

| 0 | 880 yards |
| 0 | 800 meters |

③ **Papagayo Park.** Named for the hotel that formerly occupied the grounds, Papagayo Park sits on 52 acres of prime real estate on the Costera, just after the underpass that begins at Hornos beach. Youngsters enjoy the life-size model of a Spanish galleon, made to look like the ones that once sailed into Acapulco when it was Mexico's capital of trade with the Orient. There is an aviary, a roller-skating rink, a racetrack with mite-size race cars, a replica of the space shuttle *Columbia*, bumper boats in a lagoon, and other rides. Horse and carriage rides up and down the Costera are available evenings. The two routes are from Papagayo Park to the zócalo and from Condesa Beach to the Naval base. Each costs about $5. ⊠ *Costera Miguel Alemán*, ☎ *74/85–96–23*. ☜ *No entrance fee; rides cost about 50¢ to $2.* ☉ *Daily 10–8.*

⑥ **Waterfront.** A stroll by the docks will remind you that Acapulco is still a lively commercial port and fishing center. The cruise ships anchor here, and at night Mexican parents bring their children to play on the small tree-lined promenade. Farther west, by the zócalo, are the docks for the sightseeing yachts and smaller fishing boats. It's a good spot to join the Mexicans in people-watching. ⊠ *Costera Miguel Alemán, between Calle Escudero on the west and the San Diego Fort on the east.*

⑦ **Zócalo.** You'll find the hub of downtown and Old Acapulco at this shaded plaza, overgrown with dense trees. All day it's filled with vendors, shoe-shine men, and people lining up to use the pay phones. After siesta, they drift here to meet and greet. On Sunday evenings there's often music in the bandstand. There are several cafés and newsagents selling the English-language *Mexico City News,* so tourists lodging in the area are drawn here, too. The flea market, inexpensive tailor shops, and Woolworth's (☞ Chapter 8) are nearby. The zócalo fronts **Nuestra Señora de la Soledad,** the town's modern but unusual church, with its stark-white exterior and bulb-shaped blue and yellow spires. ⊠ *Bounded by Calle Felipe Valle on the north, Calle J. Carranza on the south, Calle J. Azueta on the west, and Calle J. Carranza on the east.*

NEED A
BREAK?

Just off the zócalo, **Sanborns** attracts locals and tourists alike; many linger for hours over the newspaper and a cup of coffee. The unnamed **café** at 45 Cinco de Mayo serves *churros* every afternoon beginning at 4. This Spanish treat of fried dough dusted with sugar and dipped in hot chocolate is popular at *merienda,* which means "snack time."

3 Beaches

OST BEACHES have fine sand and gentle water, but some, such as Revolcadero and Pie de la Cuesta, have very strong undertows and surfs, so swimming is not advised. Despite an enticing appearance and claims that officials are cleaning up the bay, it remains polluted. In addition, although vending on the beach has been officially outlawed, you'll still find yourself approached by souvenir hawkers. If these things bother you, we suggest that you follow the lead of the Mexican cognoscenti and enjoy the waters at your hotel pool.

Beaches in Mexico are public, even those that seem to belong to a big hotel.

Barra Vieja

About 27 kilometers (16 miles) east of Acapulco, between Laguna de Tres Palos and the Pacific, this magnificent beach is even more inviting than Pie de la Cuesta (☞ *below*) because the drive out is much more pleasant.

Caleta and Caletilla

On the peninsula in Old Acapulco, these two beaches once rivaled La Quebrada as the main tourist area in Acapulco's heyday. Now they attract families. Motorboats to Roqueta Island (☞ Mágico Mundo Marino *in* Chapter 2) leave from here.

Condesa

Facing the middle of Acapulco Bay, this stretch of sand has more than its share of tourists, especially singles, and the beachside restaurants are convenient for bites between parasailing flights.

Hornos and Hornitos

Running from the Plaza las Glorias Paraíso to Las Hamacas hotel, these beaches are packed shoulder to shoulder on the

weekends with locals and Mexican tourists who know a
good thing: Graceful palms shade the sand, and there are
scads of casual eateries within walking distance.

Icacos

Stretching from the naval base to El Presidente hotel, this
beach is less populated than others on the Costera, and the
morning waves are especially calm.

Pie de la Cuesta

You'll need a car or cab to reach this relatively unpopu-
lated spot, about a 25-minute drive west of Acapulco,
through one of the least picturesque parts of town. A string
of rustic restaurants border the wide beach, and straw
palapas provide shade. Be aware that the Pacific water
here is dangerous for swimming.

What attracts people to Pie de la Cuesta, besides the long
expanse of beach and spectacular sunsets, is beautiful
Coyuca Lagoon, a favorite spot for waterskiing, freshwater fishing, and boat rides. The 45-square-mile lagoon has
been featured in early *Tarzan* movies, *The African Queen,*
and, more recently, *Rambo II.* You'll know it's time to leave
when the mosquitos come out in the evening.

Puerto Marqués

Tucked below the airport highway, this strand is popular with
Mexican tourists, so it tends to get crowded on weekends.
Deep-sea fishing trips leave from here, and various water sports
are available.

Revolcadero

A wide, sprawling beach next to the Vidafel, Pierre Marqués, and Princess hotels, its water is shallow but its waves
are too rough for swimming. People come here to surf and
ride horses.

4 Dining

THE TOP RESTAURANTS IN ACAPULCO can be fun for a splurge and provide very good value. Even at the best places in town, dinner rarely exceeds $50 per person, and the atmosphere and views are fantastic. Ties and jackets are out of place, but so are shorts or jeans. Unless stated otherwise, all restaurants are open daily from 6:30 or 7 PM until the last diner leaves. Several restaurants have two seatings: 6:30 for the *gringos* and 9 for the Mexican crowd, who wisely head directly to the discos after dinner to dance off the calories.

Note: Loud music blares from many restaurants along the Costera, and proprietors will aggressively try to hustle you inside with offers of drink specials. If you're looking for a hassle-free evening, it's best either to avoid this area or decide in advance precisely where you want to dine.

CATEGORY	COST*
$$$$	over $35
$$$	$25–$35
$$	$15–$25
$	under $15

per person, excluding drinks, service, and sales tax (10%)

American

$$ ✕ **Carlos 'n' Charlie's.** This is without a doubt the most popular restaurant in town; a line forms well before the 6:30 PM opening. Part of the Anderson group (with restaurants in the United States and Spain as well as Mexico), Carlos 'n' Charlie's cultivates an atmosphere of controlled craziness. Prankster waiters, a jokester menu, and eclectic decor—everything from antique bullfight photos to a tool chest of painted gadgets hanging from the ceiling—add to the chaos. The crowd is mostly young and relaxed, which is what you need to be to put up with the rush-hour traffic noise that filters up to the covered balcony where people dine. The menu straddles the border, with ribs, stuffed shrimp, and oysters among the best offerings. ⊠ *Costera Miguel Alemán 112,* ☎ *74/84–12–85 or 84–00–39. Reservations not accepted. AE, DC, MC, V.*

\$\$ ✗ **Hard Rock Cafe.** This link in the international Hard Rock chain is one of the most popular spots in Acapulco, and with good reason. The southern-style food—fried chicken, ribs, hamburgers—is very well prepared and the portions are more than ample. The taped rock music begins at noon, and a live group starts playing at 11 PM (except Tuesday). There's always a line at the small boutique on the premises, where you can buy sports clothes and accessories bearing the Hard Rock label. ⊠ *Costera Miguel Alemán 37,* ☎ *74/84–66–80. Reservations not accepted. AE, MC, V.*

Belgian

\$\$ ✗ **La Petite Belgique.** Mexican-born Yolanda Brassart,
★   who spent years in Europe studying the culinary arts, reigns in the kitchen of this small bistro. Guillermo, her Belgian husband, obviously adores his wife—and her cooking—and makes certain that the customers are happy. Diners are greeted by the enticing aromas of goose-liver pâté, home-baked breads, and apple strudel, all displayed temptingly at the entrance. The menu changes every four months but usually includes boned duck stuffed with almonds and mushrooms, and served with a white wine and mushroom sauce. ⊠ *Plaza Marbella,* ☎ *74/84–77–25. AE, DC, MC, V.*

Continental

\$\$\$\$ ✗ **Coyuca 22.** This is possibly the most expensive restau-
★   rant in Acapulco; it is certainly one of the most beautiful. Diners eat on terraces that overlook the bay from the west, on a hilltop in Old Acapulco. The understated decor consists of Doric pillars, sculptures, and large onyx flower stands near the entrance. Diners gaze down on an enormous illuminated obelisk and a small pool. The effect is that of eating in a partially restored Greek ruin sans dust. Diners can choose from two fixed menus or order à la carte. Seafood and prime ribs are house specialties. ⊠ *Av. Coyuca 22 (a 10-min taxi ride from the zócalo),* ☎ *74/82–34–68 or 74/83–50–30. Reservations essential. AE, DC, MC, V. Closed Apr. 30–Nov. 1.*

Acapulco Dining

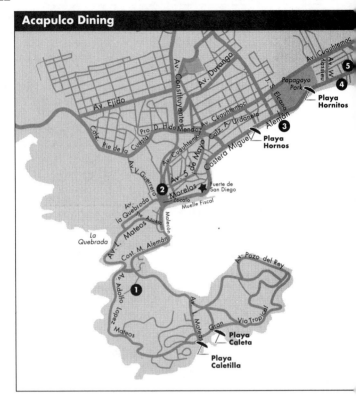

Bella Vista, **20**
Beto's, **8**
Blackbeard's, **7**
Carlos 'n'
Charlie's, **9**
Casa Nova, **21**
Coyuca 22, **1**
El Cabrito, **13**
El Olvido, **14**

Hard Rock
Café, **11**
La Casa
de Tere, **2**
La Petite
Belgique, **15**
La Vela, **22**
Los
Rancheros, **18**

Madeiras, **19**
100% Natural, **5**
Paradise, **6**
Pipo's, **12**
Sirocco, **3**
Suntory, **17**
Villa Fiore, **10**
Zapata, Villa
y Cia, **15**

Zorrito's, **4**

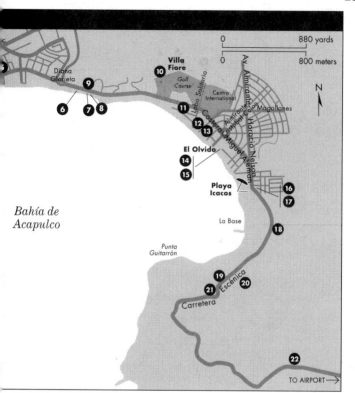

Villa
Fiore

Diana
Glorieta

Golf
Course

Centro
International

Lario Solitario

Av. Almirante

Carretera General Miguel Alemán

Almirante Horacio Nelson

Magallanes

El Olvida

Playa
Icacos

Bahía de
Acapulco

La Base

Punta
Guitarrón

Escénica

Carretera

TO AIRPORT →

880 yards

800 meters

N

$$$ ✕ **Bella Vista.** This alfresco restaurant in the exclusive Las Brisas area has fantastic sunset views of Acapulco. Its large menu offers a wide variety of dishes that range from Asian appetizers to Italian and seafood entrées. Try the delicious (and spicy!) Thai shrimp, sautéed in sesame oil, ginger, Thai chili, and hoisin sauce; or the red snapper étouffée, cooked in chardonnay, tomato, herbs, basil, and oyster sauce. ✉ *Carretera Escéncia 5255,* ☎ *74/84–15–80, ext. 500. Reservations essential. AE, DC, MC, V.*

$$$ ✕ **Madeiras.** One of Acapulco's favorite dining spots, ★ Madeiras is very difficult to get into, especially on weekends and during the Christmas and Easter holidays; many people make reservations by letter before they arrive. The bar-reception area features Art Nouveau–style chairs and startling coffee tables made of glass resting on wooden animals; the dishes and flatware were created by silversmiths in nearby Taxco; and all the tables have a view of Acapulco glittering at night. Dinner is served from a four-course, prix-fixe menu and costs about $25 without wine. Entrées include the delicious Spanish dish of red snapper in sea salt, tasty chilled soups, stuffed red snapper, and a choice of steaks and other seafood, as well as the *crepas de huitlacoche* (*huitlacoche,* or *cuitlacoche,* is a corn fungus that was a delicacy to the Aztecs). Desserts are competently prepared but have no special flair. There are seatings every 30 minutes from 7 to 10:30 PM. ✉ *Scenic Hwy. 33-B, just past La Vista shopping center,* ☎ *74/84–69–21. Reservations essential. No children under 8. AE, DC, MC, V.*

French

$$$ ✕ **El Olvido.** The view, the foliage, the Mediterranean decor, and the flickering candles combine to make this one of Acapulco's most romantic dining spots. A terraced dining area and huge windows provide all diners with a panoramic vista of the bay. French chef Daniel Janny blends the techniques of his native land with Mexican ingredients, which results in creations such as salmon roll with mango vinaigrette and quail in a honey, pineapple, and *pasilla* chili sauce. ✉ *Plaza Marbella,* ☎ *74/81–02–14. AE, DC, MC, V.*

Health Food

$ ✗ **100% Natural.** Six family-operated restaurants specialize in light, healthful food—yogurt shakes, fruit salads, and sandwiches made with whole-wheat bread. The service is quick and the food is a refreshing alternative to tacos, particularly on a hot day. Look for the green signs with white lettering. ⊠ *Costera Miguel Alemán 200, near the Acapulco Plaza,* ☎ *74/85–39–82. Another branch across from Oceanic 2000,* ☎ *74/84–84–40. No credit cards.*

Italian

$$$ ✗ **Casa Nova.** Another ultraromantic spot created by Arturo Cordova, the man behind Coyuca 22 (☞ *above*), Casa Nova is carved out of a cliff that rises up from Acapulco Bay. The views, both from the terrace and the air-conditioned interior dining room, are spectacular, the service impeccable, and the Italian cuisine divine. The menu includes antipasto, fresh pastas, a delightful *cotolette de vittello* (veal chops with mushrooms), lobster tail, and *linguini alle vongole* (linguine with clams, tomato, and garlic). ⊠ *Scenic Hwy., just past Madeiras,* ☎ *74/84–68–19. Reservations essential. AE, DC, MC, V.*

$$ ✗ **Villa Fiore.** Here, the owners of Madeiras (☞ *above*) bring you fine Italian dining under the stars in the candlelit garden of what looks like an 18th-century Venetian villa (there's also indoor seating in case of rain). Diners can choose from two fixed menus that include appetizer, soup, main course (chicken, fish, meat, or pasta), dessert, and coffee. Opt for the *calamari fritti* (fried squid in marinara sauce) as a starter, and fillet of stuffed sea bass with crab or ravioli for an entrée. Service is excellent. ⊠ *Av. del Prado 6,* ☎ *74/84–20–40. AE, DC, MC, V. Closed Wed.*

Japanese

$$$ ✗ **Suntory.** At this traditional Japanese restaurant you can dine either in a blessedly air-conditioned interior room or in the delightful Asian-style garden. It's one of the few Japanese restaurants in Acapulco and also one of the only deluxe restaurants that are open for lunch. Specialties are

the sushi and the teppan-yaki, prepared at your table by skilled chefs. ⊠ *Costera Miguel Alemán 36, across from the La Palapa hotel,* ☎ *74/84–80–88. AE, DC, MC, V.*

Mexican

$$ ✕ **Los Rancheros.** With a view of the water in the posh East Bay, here's dining at about half what you'd pay at some of the big-name places. The decor is colorful, folksy Mexican with paper streamers, checked tablecloths, and lopsided mannequins in local dress. Specials include *carne tampiqueña* (fillet of beef broiled with lemon juice), chicken enchiladas, and *queso fundido* (melted cheese served as a side dish with chips). Mariachis entertain at lunch and dinner, Thursdays through Sundays. ⊠ *Scenic Hwy. just before Extasis disco (on left as you head toward airport),* ☎ *74/84–19–08. AE, MC, V. Closed Tues.*

$$ ✕ **Zapata, Villa y Cia.** This is a Mexican version of the Hard Rock Cafe, where the music and food (excellent) are strictly Mexican and the memorabilia is Mexican Revolution, with guns, hats, and photographs of Pancho Villa. The definite highlight of an evening here is a visit from a sombrero-wearing baby burro, so be sure to bring your camera. ⊠ *Hyatt Regency, Costera Miguel Alemán 1,* ☎ *74/ 84–28–88. AE, DC, MC, V.*

$$ ✕ **Zorrito's.** When Julio Iglesias is in town, this is where he heads in the wee hours of the morning, after the discos close. He's been known to sing along with the band that's on hand to play every evening, from 6 PM on. The menu features a host of steak and beef dishes, and the special, *filete tampiqueña,* comes with tacos, enchiladas, guacamole, and frijoles. ⊠ *Costera Miguel Alemán and Anton de Alaminos, next to Banamex,* ☎ *74/85–37–35. Reservations not accepted. AE, MC, V. Closed Tues.*

$ ✕ **El Cabrito.** This is a local favorite for true Mexican cuisine and ambience. The name of the restaurant—"The Goat"—is also its specialty. In addition, you can choose among mole; jerky with egg, fish, and seafood; and other Mexican dishes. ⊠ *Costera Miguel Alemán, between Nina's and the Hard Rock,* ☎ *74/84–77–11. Reservations not accepted. MC, V.*

$ ✕ **La Casa de Tere.** Hidden in a commercial district down-
★ town (signs point the way), La Casa de Tere offers little in
the way of upscale atmosphere—beer-hall tables and chairs,
colorful Mexican decorations, and photos of Acapulco of
yore—and even less of a view, but its tasty food and low
prices make it a favorite with savvy Acapulqueños. Doña
Teresa Cabrera de Saab, who keeps a sharp eye on her spot-
lessly clean, open-air establishment, offers diners a small
but varied menu that includes an outstanding *sopa de tortilla* (tortilla soup), chicken in mole sauce, and corn cus-
tard. The *comida corrida*—which includes soup, a main dish,
and dessert—is an exceptionally good buy. Powerful overhead fans make up for the lack of air-conditioning. ⊠ *Al-
fonso Martín 1721, 2 blocks from Costera Miguel Alemán,*
☎ *74/85–77–35. Reservations not accepted. No credit
cards. Closed Mon.*

Seafood

$$$ ✕ **Blackbeard's.** Dark, with a pirate-ship motif, Black-
beard's has maps covering the tables in the cozy booths,
and the walls are adorned with wooden figureheads. Every
movie star, from Bing Crosby to Liz Taylor, who ever set
foot here has his or her photo posted in the lounge. Jumbo
portions of shrimp, steak, and lobster keep customers sat-
isfied. A disco on the premises starts throbbing at 10:30
PM. ⊠ *Costera Miguel Alemán, on Condesa Beach near the
Fiesta Americana Condesa,* ☎ *74/84–25–49. AE, MC, V.*

$$$ ✕ **La Vela.** Set on a wharf that juts out into Pichilingue
★ Bay, this open-air dining spot is protected by a dramatic
roof that simulates a huge white sail. It's very atmospheric
after dark, when a stillness hangs over the bay and the lights
of Puerto Marqués flicker in the distance. The menu features a variety of fish and shellfish dishes, but the specialty
of the house is the red snapper *à la talla* (basted with chili
and other spices and broiled over hot coals). There are no
overhead fans, and although there is usually a delightful
breeze, it can get quite uncomfortable on steamy summer
nights. ⊠ *Camino Real Acapulco Diamante, Carretera Escénica Km 14,* ☎ *74/66–10–10. AE, DC, MC, V.*

$$ ✕ **Beto's.** By day you can eat right on the beach and enjoy
live music; by night this palapa-roofed restaurant is trans-

formed into a dim and romantic dining area lighted by candles and paper lanterns. Whole red snapper, lobster, and ceviche are recommended. There is a second branch next door and a third at Barra Vieja Beach—where the specialty is *pescado à la talla* (fish spread with chili and other spices and then grilled over hot coals). Beto's Safari turns into a disco on Fridays and Saturdays after 10. ⊠ *Beto's, Costera Miguel Alemán at Condesa Beach,* ☎ *74/84–04–73. Beto's Safari, Costera Miguel Alemán, next to Beto's,* ☎ *74/84–47–62. Beto's Barra Vieja, Barra Vieja Beach, no phone. AE, MC, V.*

$$ ✕ **Paradise.** This is the leading beach-party restaurant. T-shirted waiters drop leis over your head as you arrive, hand roses to the ladies, teach dance steps, and sing tropical songs. The menu (primarily seafood) has the same number of dishes as drinks, a pretty good indicator of what this place is like. Paradise has one of the biggest dance floors in Acapulco and live music day and night. Chaos reigns at lunchtime (from 2 to 5), and the mood picks up again from 8:30 to 10:30. Expect a young crowd. ⊠ *Costera Miguel Alemán 107, next to Mimi's Chili Saloon,* ☎ *74/84–59–88. Reservations not accepted. AE, DC, MC, V.*

$$ ✕ **Pipo's.** Situated on a rather quiet part of the Costera,
★ this family-run seafood restaurant doesn't have an especially interesting view, but diners come here for the fresh fish, good service, and reasonable prices. *Huachinango veracruzano* (red snapper prepared with tomatoes, peppers, onion, and olives) and fillet of fish in *mojo de ajo* (garlic butter) are about as sophisticated as the food preparation gets. The ceviche is an Acapulco tradition, as is *vuelve à la vida,* an immense seafood cocktail that, as the name implies, is guaranteed to bring you "back to life." ⊠ *Costera Miguel Alemán and Nao Victoria, across from the Acapulco International Center,* ☎ *74/84–01–65; also downtown at Almirante Bretón 3,* ☎ *74/82–22–37. Reservations not accepted. AE, MC, V.*

Spanish

$$ ✕ **Sirocco.** This beachside eatery is numero uno for those who crave Spanish food in Acapulco. The tiled floors and

heavy wooden furniture give it a Mediterranean feel. Specialties include *pulpo en su tinta* (octopus in its own ink) and other types of seafood. Order paella (there are 10 varieties) when you arrive at the beach—it takes a half hour to prepare. ⊠ *Costera Miguel Alemán, across from Aurrerá,* ☎ *74/85–23–86 or 74/85–94–90. AE, MC, V.*

5 Lodging

ALTHOUGH ACAPULCO has been an important port since colonial times, it lacks the converted monasteries and old mansions found in Mexico City. But the Costera is chockablock with new luxury high-rises and local franchises of such major U.S. hotel chains as Hyatt and Howard Johnson. Since these hotels tend to be characterless, your choice will depend on location and what facilities are available. All major hotels can make water-sports arrangements.

In Acapulco geography is price, so where you stay determines what you pay. The most exclusive area is the Acapulco Diamante, home to some of the most expensive hotels in Mexico—so lush and well equipped that most guests don't budge from the minute they arrive. The minuses: Revolcadero Beach is too rough for swimming (though great for surfing), and this area is a 15- to 25-minute (expensive) taxi ride from the heart of Acapulco. The atmosphere of Acapulco Diamante is refined and revolves around games of golf or tennis, dining at some of Acapulco's better restaurants, and dancing at the glamorous Extravaganzza, Palladium, and Fantasy discos.

There is much more activity on Costera Miguel Alemán, where the majority of large hotels, discos, American-style restaurants, and airline offices are found, along with Acapulco's most popular beaches. All the Costera hotels have freshwater pools and sundecks, and most have restaurants and/or bars overlooking the beach, if not on the sand itself. Hotels across the street are almost always less expensive than those directly on the beach; because there are no private beaches in Acapulco, all you have to do is cross the road to enjoy the sand.

Moving west along the Costera leads you to downtown Acapulco. The beaches and restaurants here are popular with Mexican vacationers, and the dozens of hotels attract Canadian and European bargain hunters.

You can assume that accommodations that cost above $90 (double) will be air-conditioned (though you can find air-conditioned hotels for less) and will include a minibar, TV, and a view of the bay. There is usually a range of in-house restaurants and bars, as well as a pool. Exceptions exist, such as Las Brisas, which, in the name of peace and quiet, has banned TVs from all rooms. So if such extras are important to you, be sure to ask ahead. If you can't afford air-conditioning, don't panic. Even the least expensive hotels have cooling ceiling fans.

Note: Most hotels are booked solid Christmas and Easter week, so if you plan to visit then, it's wise to make reservations months in advance.

CATEGORY	COST*
$$$$	over $160
$$$	$90–$160
$$	$40–$90
$	under $40

All prices are for a standard double room, excluding 10% sales (called IVA) tax.

Acapulco Diamante

$$$$ 🏨 **Acapulco Princess.** This is the first hotel you'll see as
 ★ you leave the airport. A pyramid-shaped building flanked by two towers, the Princess has the largest capacity of any hotel in Acapulco. The hotel's fact sheet makes fascinating reading: 50 chocolate cakes are consumed daily and 2,500 staff meals are served. The Princess is one of those megahotels that are always holding at least three conventions, with an ever-present horde in the lobby checking in and greeting their fellow dentists or club members. But more rooms equals more facilities. The Princess has seven restaurants, seven bars (several of which close during the low season—April through October), a disco, tennis, golf, and shopping in a cool arcade. The pool near the reception desk is sensational—fantastic tropical ponds with little waterfalls and a slatted bridge leading into a swimming-sunning area. Rooms are light and airy, with cane furniture and rugs and curtains in colorful tropical prints. Guests can also use the facilities of the hotel's smaller sibling, the Pierre Marqués; a free shuttle bus provides transport. Accommodations include breakfast and dinner (in high season). ⊠ *Box 1351, Playa Revolcadero, 39300,* ☎ *74/69–10–00 or*

800/223–1818, FAX *74/69–10–16. 1,019 balconied rooms with bath. 7 restaurants, 7 bars, 5 pools, 2 18-hole golf courses, 11 tennis courts, exercise room, 2 basketball courts, dance club. AE, DC, MC, V.*

$$$$ ★ 🏨 **Pierre Marqués.** This hotel is doubly blessed: It is closer to the beach than any of the other East Bay hotels, and guests have access to all the Princess's facilities without the crowds. In addition, it has three pools and five tennis courts illuminated for nighttime play. Rooms are furnished identically to those at the Princess (no TVs here, however), but villas and duplex bungalows with private patios are available. Many people stay here to relax, then hit the Princess's restaurants and discos at night—the shuttle bus runs about every 10 minutes 24 hours a day. Accommodations include mandatory breakfast (breakfast and dinner during Christmas week). The Pierre is open for winter season only. ✉ *Box 1351, Playa Revolcadero, 39907,* ☎ *74/66–10–00 or 800/223–1818,* FAX *74/66–10–46. 344 rooms with bath. 2 restaurants, bar, 3 pools, 2 18-hole golf courses, 5 tennis courts. AE, DC, MC, V.*

$$$$ 🏨 **Vidafel Mayan Palace.** This all-suites resort will knock your socks off. Guests are welcomed in a 100,000-square-foot lobby that's sheltered under 75-foot palm-roofed palapas, with full-scale Maya-inspired statues surrounded by reflecting pools. The rooms, on the other hand, are surprisingly subdued. Airy and spacious, they are beautifully appointed with marble floors, light-wood furniture, sand-colored walls, original paintings, and luxurious baths; they range from a studio with hot tub (Crown Suite) to a one-bedroom with kitchenette and sitting areas (Acapulco Suite). Guests may ride a canoe or a paddleboat around the man-made, fish-filled canal that winds through the 200-acre property or swim in the 850-yard pool. ✉ *Playa Revolcadero, 39300,* ☎ *74/69–02–01 or 800/VIDAFEL,* FAX *74/62–00–08. 350 suites with bath. Restaurant, bar, 18-hole golf course, 12 lighted tennis courts, game room. AE, DC, MC, V.*

$$$$ ★ 🏨 **Westin Las Brisas.** Set high on a hillside and across the bay from most of the other main hotels, the Las Brisas hotel remains distinct in Acapulco for the secluded haven it provides its guests. This self-contained luxury complex covers 110 acres and has accommodations that range from one-bedroom units to deluxe private casitas, complete with

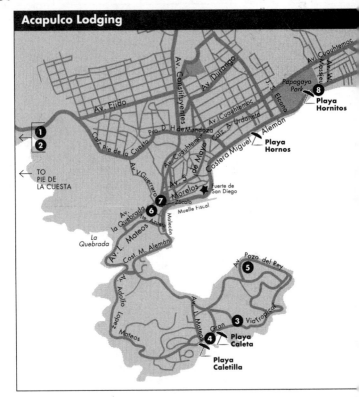

Acapulco Lodging

Acapulco Plaza, **10**	Fiesta Americana Condesa Acapulco, **12**	Hyatt Regency Acapulco, **15**	Plaza las Glorias Paraíso, **8**
Acapulco Princess, **20**	Hotel Acapulco Tortuga, **11**	Majestic, **5**	Royal El Cano, **14**
Boca Chica, **4**	Hotel Misión, **6**	Parador del Sol, **1**	Sheraton Acapulco, **16**
Camino Real Acapulco Diamante, **18**	Howard Johnson Moralisa, **9**	Pierre Marqués, **19**	Suites Alba, **3**
		Plaza las Glorias El Mirador, **7**	Ukae Kim, **2**

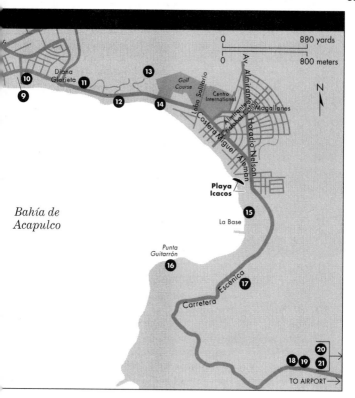

Vidafel Mayan
Palace, **21**
Villa Vera, **13**
Westin Las
Brisas, **17**

private pools that are small yet swimmable. All have beautiful bay views. Most of the facilities are open only to guests, though outsiders with a reservation may dine at the Bella Vista restaurant. Attention to detail is Las Brisas's claim to fame: Fresh hibiscus blossoms are set afloat in the pools each day, and registration takes place in a comfortable lounge, where guests are given tropical mixed drinks to sip. There are almost three employees per guest during the winter season. Transportation is by white-and-pink Jeep. You can rent one for $50 a day, including tax, gas, and insurance; or, if you don't mind a wait, the staff will do the driving. And transport is necessary—it is a good 15-minute walk to the beach restaurant, and all the facilities are far from the rooms. There is an art gallery and a few other stores. Tipping is not allowed, but a service charge of $16 a day is added to the bill. The rate includes Continental breakfast and temporary membership in the La Concha Beach Club. ⊠ *Carretera Escénica 5255, 39868,* ☎ *74/84–15–80 or 800/228–3000,* 🖷 *74/84–22–69. 300 rooms with bath. 3 restaurants, 2 bars, 3 pools (2 saltwater), hot tub, sauna, 5 tennis courts, beach. AE, DC, MC, V.*

$$$ ⊞ **Camino Real Acapulco Diamante.** Opened in 1993,
★ Acapulco's newest hotel is set at the foot of a lush tropical hillside on exclusive Pichilingue Beach, far from the madding crowd. All rooms are done in luscious pastels, with tiled floors, balcony or terrace, luxurious baths, ceiling fans, and air-conditioning. Each has a view of peaceful Puerto Marqués Bay. Rates include a buffet breakfast. ⊠ *Carretera Escénica Km 14, Calle Baja Catita, 39867,* ☎ *74/66–10–10 or 800/7–CAMINO,* 🖷 *74/66–11–11. 156 rooms. 2 restaurants, 2 bars, 3 pools, tennis court, exercise room. AE, DC, MC, V.*

$$$ ⊞ **Sheraton Acapulco.** Perfect for those who want to enjoy the sun and the sand but don't have to be in the center of everything, this Sheraton is isolated from all the hubbub of the Costera and is rather small in comparison with the chain's other properties in Mexico. The spacious, attractively decorated rooms and suites—all with private balconies, and many with sweeping views of the entire bay—are distributed among 13 villas that are set on a hillside on secluded Guitarrón Beach, 10 kilometers (6 miles) east of Acapulco proper. In order to reach your room, however, it's necessary to wait for a staff-operated funicular—a slow, sometimes frustrating procedure. The hotel's romantic fine-dining room, La Bahía, serves excellent Continental cuisine. ⊠ *Costera Guitarrón 110, 39359,* ☎ *74/81–22–22 or 800/325–3535,* FAX *74/84–37–60. 197 rooms with bath, 15 suites. 3 restaurants, 3 bars, 2 pools. AE, DC, MC, V.*

The Costera

$$$$ ⊞ **Hyatt Regency Acapulco.** Another megahotel that you never have to leave, this property is popular with business travelers and conventioneers. The entire hotel was totally refurbished in 1995, and soft pastels have been replaced with strong Caribbean colors. Tennis courts, five eateries (including a beachside seafood place, a popular Mexican dining spot, and a kosher restaurant), four bars, and a lavish shopping area are among the reasons for guests to stay put. The Hyatt is a little out of the way, a plus for those who seek quiet. To avoid the noise of the maneuvers at the neighboring naval base, ask for a room on the west side of the hotel. ⊠ *Costera Miguel Alemán 1, 39869,* ☎ *74/69–12–34 or 800/223–1234,* FAX *74/84–30–87. 690 rooms with bath. 4 restaurants, 4 bars, snack bar, 2 pools, massage, sauna, 5 tennis courts, parking (fee). AE, DC, MC, V.*

$$$$ ⊞ **Royal El Cano.** One of Acapulco's traditional favorites
★ has been completely remodeled, while still (thankfully) maintaining its '50s flavor. The interior decorators get an A+: The rooms are snappily done in white and navy blue, with white tiled floors and beautiful modern bathrooms. The only exception is the lobby, which is excruciatingly blue. There's a delightful outdoor restaurant, a more elegant indoor one, and a gorgeous pool that seems to float above the bay, with whirlpools built into its corners. Maintenance is excellent throughout the hotel. ⊠ *Costera Miguel Alemán 75, 39690,* ☎ *74/84–19–50 or 800/222–7692,* FAX *74/84–86–37. 180 rooms with bath. 2 restaurants, bar, pool. AE, DC, MC, V.*

$$$ ⊞ **Acapulco Plaza.** Although the Plaza is once again a single pyramid-shaped tower (the other two towers are now under separate management), this Fiesta Americana resort still has more facilities than many Mexican towns: four bars and an equal number of restaurants, tennis courts, a sauna, three pools, and a location next door to the Plaza Bahía, Acapulco's largest shopping mall. The lobby bar is most extraordinary—a wooden hut, suspended by a cable from the roof, reached by a gangplank from the second floor of the lobby and overlooking a garden full of flamingos and other exotic birds. Guest rooms tell the same old story—pastels and blond wood replacing passé dark greens and browns—but guests continue to be content with the facilities and service. ⊠ *Costera Miguel Alemán 123, 39670,* ☎ *74/85–90–50 or 800/FIESTA–1,* 𝐅𝐀𝐗 *74/85–54–93. 506 rooms with bath. 4 restaurants, 4 bars, 3 pools, sauna, 4 tennis courts, health club. AE, DC, MC, V.*

$$$ 🏨 **Fiesta Americana Condesa Acapulco.** Right in the thick of the main shopping-restaurant district, the Condesa, as everyone calls it, is ever popular with tour operators. The rooms and baths, which were totally redecorated in 1994, have a nice fresh look.The bathrooms have new fixtures and raspberry shower curtains; bedrooms feature hot-pink lamps, pastel bedspreads, and deep blue curtains. ⊠ *Costera Miguel Alemán 1220, 39690,* ☎ *74/84–28–28 or 800/FIESTA–1,* 𝐅𝐀𝐗 *74/84–18–28. 500 rooms with bath. 2 restaurants, bar, 2 pools. AE, DC, MC, V.*

$$ 🏨 **Hotel Acapulco Tortuga.** A helpful staff and prime location make the "Turtle Hotel" an appealing choice. It is also one of the few nonbeach hotels to have a garden (handkerchief-size), a beach club (in Puerto Marqués), and a pool where most of the guests hang out. At night the activity shifts to the piano bar. The downside of this merriment is the noise factor. The best bet is a room facing west on an upper floor. All rooms have blue-green pile rugs and small tables. Breakfast is served in the lobby café; lunch and dinner can be taken in the more formal restaurant. ⊠ *Costera Miguel Alemán 132, 39300,* ☎ *74/84–88–89 or 800/832–7491,* 𝐅𝐀𝐗 *74/84–73–85. 252 rooms with bath. 2 restaurants, coffee shop, piano bar, pool. AE, DC, MC, V.*

$$ 🏨 **Howard Johnson Maralisa.** Formerly the sister hotel
★   of the Villa Vera (☞ *below*), this hotel, located on the beach side of the Costera, is now a part of the Howard Johnson chain. The sundeck surrounding two small pools—palm trees and ceramic tiles—is unusual and picturesque. The rooms are light, decorated in whites and pastels. This is a small, friendly place; all rooms have TVs and balconies, and the price is right. ⊠ *Box 721, Calle Alemania, 39670,* ☎ *74/85–66–77 or 800/IGO–HOJO,* 𝐅𝐀𝐗 *74/85–92–28. 90*

rooms with bath. Restaurant, bar, 2 pools, beach. AE, DC, MC, V.

$$ 🖼 **Plaza Las Glorias Paraíso.** The last of the big Costera hotels is a favorite of tour groups, so the lobby is forever busy. The rooms look brighter and roomier since the management replaced the heavy Spanish-style furniture with light woods and pastels. Guests lounge by the pool or at the beachside restaurant by day. The pool area is rather small and the beach can get crowded, but the restaurants are exceptionally good and the staff couldn't be nicer. Book early for high season, which is prime time for the tour groups. ⊠ *Costera Miguel Alemán 163, 39670,* ☎ *74/85–55–96 or 800/342–AMIGO,* 🖷 *74/82–45–64. 422 rooms with bath. 2 restaurants, bar, coffee shop, pool, sauna. AE, DC, MC, V.*

$$ 🖼 **Villa Vera.** A five-minute drive north of the Costera leads to what was once one of Acapulco's most exclusive hotels. Some of the villas, which were once private homes, have their own pools. Standard rooms, in pastels and white, are not especially large. No matter. No one spends much time in the rooms. The main pool, with its swim-up bar, is the hotel's hub. By night guests dine at the terraced restaurant, with its stunning view of the bay. There's an exercise facility, and two championship tennis courts host the Celebrity and Veterans tennis tournaments. ⊠ *Box 560, Lomas del Mar 35, 39690,* ☎ *74/84–03–33,* 🖷 *74/84–74–79. 74 rooms with bath. Restaurant, piano bar, pools, beauty salon, massage, sauna, 2 tennis courts. AE, MC, V.*

Old Acapulco

$$$ 🖼 **Boca Chica.** This small hotel is in a secluded area on a
★ small peninsula, and its terraced rooms overlook the bay and Roqueta Island. It's a low-key place that's a favorite of Mexico City residents in the know. There's a private beach club with a natural saltwater pool for guests and a seafood, sushi, and oyster bar. Accommodations include mandatory breakfast and dinner in high season. ⊠ *Caletilla Beach, 39390,* ☎ *74/83–67–41,* 🖷 *74/83–95–13. 40 rooms. Restaurant, seafood bar, 2 pools. AE, DC, MC, V.*

$$ 🖼 **Plaza las Glorias El Mirador.** The old El Mirador has been taken over by the Plaza las Glorias chain, which is part of the Sidek conglomerate responsible for marina and golf developments all over Mexico. Very Mexican in style—white with red tiles—the Plaza las Glorias is set high on a hill with a spectacular view of Acapulco and of the cliff divers performing at La Quebrada. ⊠ *Quebrada 74, 39300,* ☎ *74/83–11–55 or 800/342–AMIGO,* ℻ *74/82–45–64. 143 rooms with bath. 2 restaurants, 3 pools. AE, DC, MC, V.*

$$ 🖭 **Suites Alba.** Situated on a quiet hillside in "Acapulco Tradicional," the Alba is a resort-style hotel that offers bargain prices. All suites are air-conditioned and have a kitchenette, private bath, and terrace. There is no extra charge for up to two children under 12 sharing a room with relatives, which makes it especially popular with families. Caleta and Caletilla beaches are within walking distance, and the hotel has a beach club at Caleta with a 330-foot toboggan. ⊠ *Grand Via Tropical 35, 39390,* ☎ *74/83–00–73,* ℻ *74/83–83–78. 283 rooms. 3 restaurants, bar, grocery, 3 pools, tennis court, beach. AE, DC, MC, V.*

$ 🖭 **Hotel Misión.** Two minutes from the zócalo, this attractive budget hotel is the only colonial-style hotel in Acapulco. The English-speaking family that runs the Misión lives in a traditional house built in the 19th century. A newer structure housing the guest rooms was added in the 1950s. It surrounds a greenery-rich courtyard with an outdoor dining area. The rooms are small and by no means fancy, with bare cement floors and painted brick walls. But every room has a shower, and there is even hot water. The Misión appears in several European guidebooks, so expect a Continental clientele. The best rooms are on the second and third floors; the top-floor room is large but hot in the daytime. ⊠ *Calle Felipe Valle 12, 39300,* ☎ *74/82–36–43. 27 rooms, showers only. No credit cards.*

$ 🖭 **Majestic.** This dowager hotel was totally renovated in
★ 1995. The electric-blue postmodern exterior is somewhat shocking, but the stunning decor of the spacious rooms—tile floors, cool colors, and good lighting—is completely unexpected in a hotel in this price category. Entrance is through the seventh-floor lobby, and the rest of the hotel is terraced down a rocky cliff (in fact, seen from the Costera Miguel Alemán, the Majestic has often been described as looking like a typewriter). The rooms in the main building each have air-conditioning, cable TV, private terrace, a double bed,

and two studio couches; the villa rooms are smaller. There is no beach at the hotel, but free transportation is provided to the hotel's beach club, which is located next to the Club de Yates. An all-inclusive plan is also available. ⊠ *Av. Pozo del Rey 74, 39390,* ☎ *74/83–227–13,* FAX *74/82–16–14. 200 rooms. 2 restaurants, 2 bars, 2 pools, tennis court, beach club, dance club, parking. AE, DC, MC, V.*

Pie de la Cuesta

$$$ ⊞ **Parador del Sol.** Traversing both the lagoon and the
★ Pacific Ocean sides of the Pie de la Cuesta road, this all-inclusive property gives the impression that it was designed as a luxury resort. The 150 rooms are distributed among pink villas that are scattered over some 1,100 square feet of gardens. Spacious, with tile floors and baths, each room is air-conditioned and equipped with color TV, phone, and a fan-cooled terrace complete with hammocks. The rate includes all meals and refreshments, domestic drinks, tennis, and nonmotorized water sports. ⊠ *Km 5 Carretera Pie de la Cuesta–Barra de Coyuca, Box 1070, 39300,* ☎ *74/60–20–03,* FAX *74/60–16–49. 150 rooms with bath. Restaurant, 2 bars, 2 pools, miniature golf, 4 tennis courts, health club, dance club. AE, DC, MC, V.*

$ ⊞ **Ukae Kim.** A cluster of 10 junior suites that is especially popular with Europeans and Canadians, Ukae Kim is set among towering palms on Acapulco's famous "sunset" beach, just across the road from the tranquil Coyuca Lagoon. The charming rooms are fitted with canopied beds, sitting areas, and Mexican tiled baths, and although the furnishings are a bit worn, a fresh coat of bright pink paint gives the place a festive air. The rooms on the beach aren't air-conditioned, but there is generally enough of a breeze to make them comfortable. ⊠ *Av. Pie de la Cuesta 358,* ☎ *74/60–21–87,* FAX *74/60–21–88. 10 rooms with bath. Restaurant, pool. No credit cards.*

6 Nightlife and the Arts

ACAPULCO HAS ALWAYS been famous for its nightlife. The minute the sun slips over the horizon, the Costera comes alive with people milling around window-shopping, deciding where to dine, and generally biding their time till the disco hour. If you'd rather conserve your energy than practice the high art of disco-hopping, there are live shows and folk-dance performances. The big resorts have live music to accompany the early-evening happy hour, and some feature big-name bands from the United States for less than you would pay at home. There is nightly entertainment at most hotels, some of which sponsor theme parties—Italian Night, Beach Party Night, and similar festivities.

Cultural Shows

The Acapulco International Center (⊠ Costera Miguel Aleman, ☎ 74/84–70–50), also known as the Convention Center, has a Mexican fiesta Wednesday and Friday; it features mariachi bands, singers, and the "Flying Indians" from Papantla. The show with dinner and drinks costs about $20, entrance to the show alone is $10, and the performance with open bar is $12. The buffet dinner starts at 7:15, the performance at 8. On Friday, Cantina Night at El Mexicano restaurant in **Westin Las Brisas** hotel, the fiesta starts off with a *tianguis* (marketplace) of handicrafts and ends with a spectacular display of fireworks.

Dance

Nina's (⊠ Costera Miguel Alemán 2909, ☎ 74/84–24–00) is a combination dance hall and disco where the bands play salsa and other Latin rhythms. There's a live show—mostly impersonations of famous entertainers—at 12:45.

Discos

Reservations are advisable for a big group, and late afternoon or after 9 PM are the best times to call. New Year's Eve requires advance planning.

Except for Pyramid Club, Palladium, Fantasy, and Extravaganzza, all the discos are clustered on the Costera.

Baby O, an old favorite, packs them in even in the middle of the week. Eschewing the glitz and mirrors of most discos in Acapulco, Baby O resembles a cave in a tropical jungle. The crowd is 18–30 and mostly tourists, although many Mexicans come here, too. In fact, this is one of Acapulco's legendary pickup spots, so feel free to ask someone to dance. When the pandemonium gets to you, retreat to the little hamburger restaurant. ⊠ *Costera Miguel Alemán 22,* ☎ *74/84–74–74.*

Discobeach is Acapulco's only alfresco disco and its most informal one. The under-30 crowd sometimes even turns up in shorts. The waiters are young and friendly—some people find them overly so. One night they're all in togas carrying bunches of grapes; the next they're in pajamas. Every Wednesday, ladies' night, all the women receive flowers. "Sex on the Beach"—rum, vodka, Cointreau, fruit juice, and grenadine (don't say you weren't warned!)—is the house specialty, in all senses of the word. This is a very popular place. ⊠ *On Condesa Beach,* ☎ *74/84–70–64.*

Extravaganzza vies with Palladium for first place as Acapulco's most splendiferous disco, boasting the ultimate in light and sound. It accommodates 700 at a central bar and in comfortable booths, and a glass wall provides an unbelievably breathtaking view of Acapulco Bay. No food is served, but Los Rancheros is just a few steps away. The music (which is for all ages) starts at 10:30. ⊠ *On the Scenic Hwy. to Las Brisas,* ☎ *74/84–71–64.*

Fantasy is one of the most exclusive of all the discos in Acapulco. If there are any celebrities in town, they'll be here, rubbing elbows with or bumping into local fashion designers and artists—since Fantasy is quite snug, to put it nicely. This is one of the only discos where people really dress up, with the men in well-cut pants and shirts and the women in racy outfits and cocktail dresses. The crowd is 25–50 and mainly in couples. Singles gravitate toward the two bars in the back. A line sometimes forms, so people come here earlier than they do to other places. By midnight the dance floor is so packed that people dance on the wide windowsills that look out over the bay. At 2 AM there is a fireworks display. A glassed-in elevator provides an interesting overview of the scene and leads upstairs to a little shop that stocks T-shirts and lingerie. ⊠ *On the Scenic Hwy., next to Las Brisas,* ☎ *74/84–67–27.*

Hard Rock Cafe, filled with rock memorabilia, is part bar, part restaurant, part dance hall, and part boutique (☞ Chapter 4).

News is enormous, with seating for 1,200 people in love seats and booths. The most popular nights are Wednesday and Friday, when everyone is bathed in foam, with a kind of wet-T-shirt effect. From 10:30 (opening time) to 11:30, the music is slow and romantic; then the disco music and the light show begin, and they go on till dawn. ⊠ *Costera Miguel Alemán 3308, across from the Hyatt Regency,* ☎ *74/84–59–02.*

Palladium, inaugurated at the end of 1993, proves that Acapulco remains the disco capital of the world. Extravaganzza creator Tony Rullán has produced another spectacle: a waterfall that cascades down the hill from the dance-floor level and makes this place hard to miss. As at Extravaganzza, the dance floor is nearly surrounded by 50-foot-high windows, giving dancers a spectacular view of all Acapulco. ⊠ *On the Scenic Hwy. to Las Brisas,* ☎ *74/81–03–30.*

Pyramid Club, a combination disco and video bar designed to look like a 21st-century Aztec pyramid and equipped with the last word in sound systems, has replaced Tiffany, the posh disco at the Princess Hotel. ⊠ *Princess Hotel,* ☎ *74/69–10–00.*

7 Outdoor Activities and Sports

Participant Sports

A place of leisure, Acapulco still offers an abundance of activities for those seeking anything from fun in the sun to serious workouts. Bars and restaurants line many beaches, so be careful not to mix alcohol consumption with water sports. Sunscreen protection during your outdoor day activities will prevent the pains of sunburn from affecting your disco dancing in the evening.

Fishing

Fishing trips can be arranged through your hotel, downtown at the Pesca Deportiva near the *muelle* (dock) across from the zócalo, or through travel agents. At the docks near the zócalo you can hire a boat for $30 a day (two lines). It is safer to stick with one of the reliable companies whose boats and equipment are in good condition. Boats accommodating 4 to 10 people cost $180–$500 a day, $45–$60 by chair. Excursions usually leave about 7 AM and return at 1 or 2 PM. You are required to get a fishing license ($7) from the Secretaría de Pesca; you'll find their representative at the dock. Don't show up during siesta, between 2 and 4 in the afternoon.

For deep-sea fishing, **Divers de México** (☞ Scuba Diving, *below*) has well-maintained boats for 4 to 10 passengers for $200 to $500. It also offers private yacht charters. Small boats for freshwater fishing can be rented at **Cadena's** and **Tres Marías** at Coyuca Lagoon.

Fitness and Swimming

Most of the time, Acapulco weather is like August in the warmest parts of the United States. This means that you should cut back on your workouts and maintain proper hydration by drinking plenty of water.

Acapulco Princess Hotel offers the best hotel fitness facilities, including a gym with stationary bikes, Universal machines, and free weights. Because the Princess is about 15 kilometers (9 miles) from the city center and the pollution of Acapulco, you can even swim in the ocean here if you beware of the strong undertow.

Villa Vera Spa and Fitness Center (⊠ Lomas del Mar 35, ☎ 74/84–03–33) has a modern spa and fitness center and is equipped with exercise machines (including step machines), free weights, and benches. Masseuses and cosmetologists give facials and massages inside or by the pool, as you wish. Both the beauty center and the gym are open to nonguests.

Westin Las Brisas is where you should stay if you like to swim but don't like company or competition. Individual casitas come with private, or semiprivate, pools; the beach club has two saltwater pools (☞ Chapter 5, for both). Most of the major hotels in town along the Costera Miguel Alemán also have pools.

Golf

Two 18-hole championship golf courses are shared by the **Princess** and **Pierre Marqués** hotels. Reservations should be made in advance (☎ 74/84–31–00). Greens fees are $60 for guests and $80 for nonguests. A round at the 18-hole **Vidafel** (☎ 74/69–02–01) course is $70 for nonguests. There is also a public golf course at the **Club de Golf** (☎ 74/84–07–81) on the Costera across from the Acapulco Malibú hotel. Greens fees are $16 for 9 holes, $25 for 18 holes. The links at Tres Vidas and Diamante Country Club are reserved for members and their guests.

Horseback Riding

A gallop on Revolcadero Beach can be arranged through the **Charro Association** (✉ Costera Miguel Alemán 137, ☎ 74/85–64–67). Round-trip transportation to Revolcadero, a guide, and an hour on a sturdy mount should run you about $30.

Jogging

If you don't like beach jogging, the only real venue for running in the downtown area is along the sidewalk next to the Costera Miguel Alemán at the seafront, but you'll have to go very early, before traffic fumes set in. Away from the city center, the best area for running is out at the Acapulco Princess Hotel, on the airport road. A 2-kilometer (1-mile) loop is laid out along a lightly traveled road, and in the early morning you can also run along the asphalt trails on the golf course.

Scuba Diving

Arnold Brothers (⊠ Costera Miguel Alemán 205, ☏ 74/82–18–77) also runs daily scuba-diving excursions and snorkeling trips. The scuba trips cost $25 and last for 2 to 2½ hours.

Divers de México (⊠ downtown near the Fiesta and Bonanza yachts, ☏ 74/82–13–98), owned by a helpful and efficient American woman, provides English-speaking captains and comfortable American-built yachts. A three- to four-hour scuba-diving excursion—including equipment, lessons in a pool for beginners, and drinks—costs about $55 per person. If you are a certified diver, the excursion is $45.

Tennis

Court fees range from about $3 to $20 an hour during the day and are 15% more in the evening. At the hotel courts, nonguests pay about $5 more per hour. Lessons with English-speaking instructors start at about $10 an hour; ball boys get a $2 tip.

Places in town to play tennis include **Acapulco Plaza** (☏ 74/85–90–50), four hard-surface courts, two lighted; **Acapulco Princess** (☏ 74/69–10–00), two indoor courts, nine outdoor; **Club de Tennis and Golf** (⊠ Costera Miguel Alemán, across from Hotel Malibu, ☏ 74/84–07–81); **Hyatt Regency** (☏ 74/69–12–34), five lighted courts; **Pierre Marqués** (☏ 74/66–10–00), five courts; **Tiffany's Racquet Club** (⊠ Av. Villa Vera 120, ☏ 74/84–79–49), five courts; and **Villa Vera Hotel** (☏ 74/84–03–33), two outdoor lighted clay courts.

Water Sports

Waterskiing, broncos (one-person motorboats), and parasailing can all be arranged on the beach. Parasailing is an Acapulco highlight and looks terrifying until you actually try it. Most people who do it love the view and go back again and again. An eight-minute trip costs $12. Waterskiing is about $30 an hour; broncos cost $20 an hour. Windsurfing can be arranged at Caleta and most of the beaches along the Costera but is especially good at Puerto Marqués. At Coyuca Lagoon, you can try your hand (or feet) at barefoot waterskiing. The main surfing beach is Revolcadero.

Spectator Sports

Bullfights

The season runs from Christmas to Easter, and *corridas* are held on Sunday at 5:30. Tickets are available through your hotel or at the **Plaza de Toros** ticket window (⊠ Av. Circunvalación, across from Caleta Beach, ☎ 74/82–11–81) Monday–Saturday 10–2 and Sunday 10:30–5. Tickets cost $12, and a $14 seat in the first five rows—in the shade (*sombra*)—is worth the extra cost. Preceding the fight are performances of Spanish dances and music by the Chili Frito band.

Jai Alai

The **Jai Alai Acapulco Race & Sports Book** (⊠ Costera Miguel Alemán 498, ☎ 74/81–16–50) has a capacity for 1,500 spectators. The fast-paced games take place Tuesday through Sunday at 9 PM, December through September. Entrance is $7, but $4 is reimbursed with your first bet. In addition to bets on jai alai, bets are taken on all major sports events—basketball, football, baseball, boxing, horse and greyhound racing—that are transmitted directly via satellite.

8 Shopping

THE MAIN SHOPPING STRIP is on Costera
Miguel Alemán from the Acapulco Plaza
to the El Presidente Hotel. Here you can
find Guess, Peer, Aca Joe, Amarras, Polo Ralph Lauren, and
other fashionable sportswear boutiques. Downtown (Old)
Acapulco doesn't have many name shops, but this is where
you'll find the inexpensive tailors patronized by the Mexicans, lots of little souvenir shops, and a vast flea market
with crafts. Also downtown are Woolworth's and Sanborns. Most shops are open from 10 to 7 Monday through
Saturday and close on Sunday.

Department Stores and Supermarkets

Except for the waitresses' uniforms, the food, and a good
handicrafts selection, **Sanborns** is very un-Mexican. Still,
it is an institution throughout Mexico. It sells English-language newspapers, magazines, and books, as well as a line
of high-priced souvenirs. This is a useful place to come for
postcards, cosmetics, and medicines. Sanborns' restaurants
are popular for their *enchiladas suizas* (prepared with lots
of cream and cheese), *molletes* (toasted rolls spread with
refried beans and cheese), their seven-fruit drink, and their
slow service. The Estrella del Mar branch (⊠ Costera
Miguel Alemán 1226, ☎ 74/84–44–13) and the downtown
branch (⊠ Costera Miguel Alemán 209, ☎ 74/82–61–67)
are both open from 7 AM to midnight during the high season and from 7 AM to 11 PM during the low season.

Branches of **Aurrerá, Gigante, Price Club, Sam's,** and Acapulco's original supermarket, fittingly called **Super-Super,**
are all on the Costera and sell everything from lightbulbs
and newspapers to bottles of tequila and postcards. If you
are missing anything at all, you should be able to pick it
up at these stores or at the **Comercial Mexicana,** which has
three branches (⊠ Av. Farallón 216, near the Diana; Costera
Miguel Alemán 243, downtown; Av. Ruiz Cortines 13).

Woolworth's (⊠ Escudero 250 in Old Acapulco) is much
like the five-and-dime stores found all over the United
States, but with a Mexican feel.

Malls

Malls in Acapulco range from the delightful air-conditioned shopping arcade at the Princess hotel to rather gloomy collections of shops that sell cheap jewelry and embroidered dresses. Malls are listed below from east to west.

On the Costera, across from the Fiesta Americana Condesa hotel, is the **Plaza Condesa,** which offers a cold-drink stand, an Italian restaurant, a gym and weight-training center, and a greater concentration of silver shops than you'll find anywhere else in Acapulco. The multilevel **Marbella Mall,** at the Diana Glorieta, features Martí, a well-stocked sporting-goods store, and Bing's Ice Cream, as well as several restaurants. **Aca Mall,** which is next door, is all white and marble; here you'll find Polo Ralph Lauren, Ferrioni, Aca Joe, and another Martí.

Plaza Bahía, next to the Acapulco Plaza hotel, is a place for serious shopping. It is a huge, completely enclosed and air-conditioned mall where you could easily spend an entire day. Stores include Dockers, Benetton, Nautica, and Ferrioni, for chic casual wear for men and women; Ragazza, which carries an exquisite line of fine lingerie; Aspasia, which offers locally designed, glitzy evening dresses and chunky diamanté jewelry; Bally for shoes; restaurants and snack bars; and a video-game arcade.

Markets

The **Mercado Municipal,** a good place to shop for crafts, is described in Chapter 2.

El Mercado de Artesanías, a conglomeration of every souvenir in town, is a 20-minute walk from the zócalo. You'll find fake ceremonial masks, the ever-present onyx chessboards, $15 hand-embroidered dresses, imitation silver, hammocks, ceramics, even skin cream made from turtles (don't buy it, because turtles are endangered and you won't get it through U.S. Customs). The market is open daily 9–9. ☒ *To get to the market from the zócalo, turn left as you leave Woolworth's and continue to the Multibanco Comermex. Turn right, go one block, and then turn left; when you reach the Banamex, you'll see the market on your right.*

In an effort to get the itinerant vendors off the beaches and streets, the local government set up a series of **flea markets** along the Costera, mostly uninviting dark tunnels of stalls that carry what seems to be an inexhaustible supply of inexpensive collectibles and souvenirs, including serapes, ceramics, straw hats, shell sculptures, carved walking canes, and wooden toys. The selections of archaeological-artifact replicas, bamboo wind chimes, painted wooden birds (from $5 to $30 each), shell earrings, and embroidered clothes begin to look identical. Prices at the flea markets are often quite low, but it's a good idea to compare prices of items you're interested in with prices in the shops, and bargaining is essential. It's best to buy articles described as being made from semiprecious stones or silver in reputable establishments. If you don't, you may find that the beautiful jade or lapis lazuli that was such a bargain was really cleverly painted paste, or that the silver was simply a facsimile called *alpaca*.

Specialty Shops

Art

Edith Matison's Art Gallery (⊠ Costera Miguel Alemán 2010, across from the Club de Golf, ☎ 74/84–30–84) shows the works of renowned international and Mexican artists, including Calder, Dalí, Siquieros and Tamayo. **Galería Rudic** (⊠ Yañez Pinzón 9, across from the Continental Plaza, ☎ 74/84–48–44) is one of the best galleries in town, with a good collection of top contemporary Mexican artists, including Armando Amaya, Leonardo Nierman, Norma Goldberg, Trinidad Osorio, and Casiano García. **Pal Kepenyes** (⊠ Guitarrón 140, ☎ 74/84–37–38) continues to receive good press for his sculpture and jewelry, on display in his workshop. The whimsical painted papier-mâché and giant ceramic sculptures of **Sergio Bustamante** (⊠ Costera Miguel Alemán 120-9, across from the Fiesta American Condesa hotel, ☎ 74/84–49–92), can be seen at his gallery.

Boutiques

KOS (⊠ Costera Miguel Alemán, outside entrance to the Fiesta Americana Condesa del Mar hotel, ☎ 74/81–24–

34; Acapulco Plaza Hotel, ☎ 74/85–25–15) carries a sensational line of swimsuits for equally sensational bodies. **Nautica** (✉ Plaza Bahía, ☎ 74/85–75–11; smaller shop at Las Brisas hotel, ☎ 74/84–16–50) is a boutique stocked with stylish casual clothing for men. **Pasarela** (✉ Galerís Acapulco Plaza, at the entrance to Acapulco Plaza hotel, ☎ 74/85–00–17) carries its own line of gauzy dresses with a Mexican flavor, as well as some interesting accessories. **Pit** (✉ Princess arcade, ☎ 74/69–10–00) offers a smashing line of beach cover-ups and hand-painted straw hats, as well as bathing suits and light dresses.

Custom-Designed Clothes

Benny (✉ Costera Miguel Alemán 114, across from the Torres Gemelas Condominium, ☎ 74/84–15–47; downtown at Ignacio de la Llave 2, local 10, ☎ 74/82–22–28), known for years for his custom-designed resort wear for men, now caters to women as well.

Esteban's (✉ Costera Miguel Alemán 2010, across from the Club de Golf, ☎ 74/84–30–84) is the most glamorous shop in Acapulco, boasting a clientele of international celebrities and many of the important local families. Estaban's made-to-order clothes are formal and fashionable; his opulent evening dresses range from $200 to $3,000, though daytime dresses average $100. The real bargains are on the second floor, where some items are marked down as much as 80%. If you scour the racks, you can find something for $10 to $15. Esteban has a back room filled with designer clothes.

Handicrafts

AFA (✉ Horacio Nelson and James Cook, near the Hyatt Regency, ☎ 74/84–80–39) is a huge shop offering a vast selection of jewelry, handicrafts, clothing, and leather goods from all over Mexico. **La Placita** (✉ Plaza Bahía, no phone) comprises two shops designed to look like flea-market stalls. Top-quality merchandise is on display, including papier-mâché fruits and vegetables, Christmas ornaments, wind chimes, and brightly painted wooden animals from Oaxaca.

Silver and Jewelry

Antoinette (✉ Acapulco Princess shopping arcade, ☎ 74/69–10–00) has gold jewelry of impeccable design, set with precious and semiprecious stones, that you wouldn't be surprised to find on Fifth Avenue. Also on display is Emilia Castillo's line of brightly colored porcelain ware, inlaid with silver fish, stars, and birds. It's worth going to window-shop, even if you know you won't buy anything.

Suzette's (✉ Hyatt Regency hotel, ☎ 74/69–12–34), a tony shop that's been around for years, has a very laudable selection of gold jewelry.

Tane (✉ Hyatt Regency hotel, ☎ 74/84–63–48; Las Brisas hotel, ☎ 74/81–08–16) carries small selections of the exquisite flatware, jewelry, and objets d'art created by one of Mexico's most prestigious (and expensive) silversmiths.

In case you want to see the world.

At American Express, we're here to make your journey a smooth one. So we have over 1,700 travel service locations in over 120 countries ready to help. What else would you expect from the world's largest travel agency?

do more ®

http://www.americanexpress.com/travel

Travel

In case you want to be welcomed there.

We're here to see that you're always welcomed at establishments everywhere. That's why millions of people carry the American Express® Card – for peace of mind, confidence, and security, around the world or just around the corner.

do more

AMERICAN EXPRESS

Cards

In case you're running low.

We're here to help with more than 118,000 Express Cash locations around the world. In order to enroll, just call American Express before you start your vacation.

do more

And just in case.

We're here with American Express® Travelers Cheques
and Cheques *for Two.*® They're the safest way to carry
money on your vacation and the surest way to get a
refund, practically anywhere, anytime.
Another way we help you...

do more

AMERICAN
EXPRESS

**Travelers
Cheques**

9 Side Trips

TAXCO, THE SILVER CITY

IT'S A PICTURE-POSTCARD LOOK—Mexico in its Sunday best: white stucco buildings nuzzling cobblestoned streets, red-tiled roofs, and geranium-filled window boxes bright in the sun. Taxco (pronounced *tahss*-co), a colonial treasure that the Mexican government declared a national monument in 1928, tumbles onto the hills of the Sierra Madre in the state of Guerrero. Its silver mines drew foreign mining companies here for centuries. Now its charm, mild temperatures, sunshine, flowers, and silversmiths make Taxco a popular tourist destination.

Hernán Cortés discovered Taxco's mines in 1522. The silver rush lasted until the next century, when excitement tapered off. Then in the 1700s a Frenchman, who Mexicanized his name to José de la Borda, discovered a rich lode that revitalized the town's silver industry and made him exceedingly wealthy. After Borda, however, Taxco's importance faded, until the 1930s and the arrival of William G. Spratling, a writer-architect from New Orleans. Enchanted by Taxco and convinced of its potential as a silver center, Spratling set up an apprentice shop, where his artistic talent and his fascination with pre-Columbian design combined to produce silver jewelry and other artifacts that soon earned Taxco its worldwide reputation as the Silver City. Spratling's inspiration lives on in his students and their descendants, many of whom are the city's current silversmiths.

Exploring Taxco

Numbers in the margin correspond to points of interest on the Taxco Exploring map.

❶ The **Church of San Sebastián and Santa Prisca** has dominated Plaza Borda—one of the busiest and most colorful town squares in all of Mexico—since the 18th century. Usually just called Santa Prisca, it was built by French silver magnate José de la Borda in thanks to the Almighty for his having literally stumbled upon a rich silver vein. The style of the church—sort of Spanish baroque meets rococo—is known as Churrigueresque, and its pink exterior is a stunning surprise. This is one of Mexico's most beautiful colonial churches and Taxco's most important landmark. ⊠ *Southwest side of Plaza Borda.*

NEED A
BREAK?

Around Plaza Borda are several *neverías* where you can treat yourself to an ice cream in exotic flavors such as tequila, corn, avocado, or coconut. **Bar Paco's,** directly across the street from Santa Prisca, is a Taxco institution; its terrace is the perfect vantage point for watching the comings and goings on the zócalo while sipping a margarita or a beer.

---

❷ The former home of William G. Spratling houses the **Spratling Museum.** This small gallery explains the working of colonial mines and displays Spratling's collection of pre-Columbian artifacts. ⊠ *Porfirio Delgado and El Arco,* ☎ *762/2–16–60.* ⊡ *Small entrance fee.* ⊙ *Tues.–Sat. 10–5, Sun. 10–3.*

❸ **Casa Humboldt** was named for the German adventurer Alexander von Humboldt, who stayed here in 1803. The Moorish-style 18th-century house has a finely detailed facade. It now houses a wonderful little museum of colonial art. ⊠ *Calle Juan Ruíz Alarcón 6,* ☎ *762/2–55–01.* ⊡ *Small entrance fee.* ⊙ *Tues.–Sat. 10–5, Sun. 10–3.*

If you want to experience a typical Mexican market, with ❹ everything from peanuts to electrical appliances, the **Municipal Market** is worth a visit. On Saturday and Sunday mornings, when locals from surrounding towns come with their produce and crafts, the market spills out onto the surrounding streets. You'll find it directly down the hill from Santa Prisca.

The largest caverns in Mexico, the **Caves of Cacahuamilpa** (Grutas de Cacahuamilpa) are about 15 minutes northeast of Taxco. These 15 large chambers comprise 12 kilometers (8 miles) of geological formations of stalactites and stalagmites. Only some caves are illuminated. Historically, the caves were once shelter to bandits seeking refuge from justice—and others seeking refuge from injustice. Plans to turn the caves into a dinosaur park have, thankfully, been laid to rest. A guide can be hired at the entrance.

60

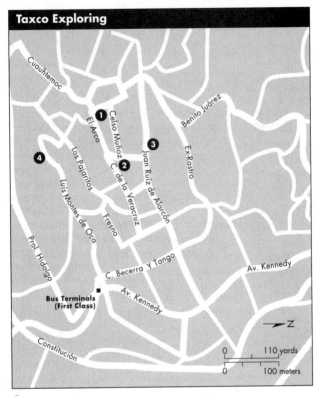

Casa
Humboldt, **3**

Church of San
Sebastián and
Santa Prisca, **1**

Municipal
Market, **4**

Spratling
Museum, **2**

Dining and Lodging

Gastronomes can find everything from tagliatelle to iguana in Taxco restaurants, and meals are much less expensive than in Acapulco. Dress is casual, but less so than at the resorts. There are several categories of hotel to choose from within Taxco's two types: the small inns nestled on the hills skirting the zócalo and the larger, more modern hotels on the outskirts of town.

$$ ✕ **La Ventana de Taxco.** The Italian recipes of manager Mario Cavagna, coupled with Mexican specialties and a fantastic view, still draw an enthusiastic crowd to this restaurant, in spite of its location in what has become an unattractive neighborhood. ⊠ *Hacienda del Solar Hotel, Hwy. 95, south of town,* ☎ *762/2–05–87. Reservations essential on weekends. AE, MC, V.*

$$ ✕ **Pagaduría del Rey.** This restaurant has a long-stand-
★ ing reputation for Continental fare served in comfortable surroundings. ⊠ *Calle H. Colegio Militar 8 (Colonia Cerro de la Bermeja, south of town),* ☎ *762/2–34–67. MC, V.*

$$ ✕ **Toni's.** Prime rib and lobster are the specialties. There's also a great view and a romantic setting. ⊠ *Monte Taxco Hotel,* ☎ *762/2–13–00. AE, DC, MC, V.*

$ ✕ **Cielito Lindo.** This charming restaurant features a Mex-ican-international menu. Give the Mexican specialties a try—for example, *pollo en pipian verde,* a chicken simmered in a mild, pumpkin-seed–based sauce. ⊠ *Plaza Borda 14,* ☎ *762/2–06–03. Reservations not accepted. MC, V.*

$ ✕ **Hosterí El Adobe.** The lack of view (there are only two
★ window tables) is more than made up for by the original decor—for example, hanging lamps made of a cluster of masks—and the excellent food. Favorites include the gar-lic-and-egg soup and the *queso adobe* (fried cheese served on a bed of potato skins and covered with a green tomatillo sauce). ⊠ *Plazuela de San Juan 13,* ☎ *762/2–14–16. MC, V.*

$ ✕ **Pizza Pazza.** All nine varieties of pizza served here are
★ tasty, but for a real treat order the *pozole norteño,* a spicy pork and hominy soup that comes with pork cracklings, chopped onion, lemon, and avocado. This cozy place, with scotch-plaid tablecloths and flowering plants, overlooks

Plaza Borda. ✉ *Calle del Arco 1,* ☎ *762/2–55–00. Reservations not accepted. MC, V.*

$ ✕ **Santa Fe.** Mexican family-type cooking at its best is served in this simple place. Puebla-style mole, Cornish hen in garlic butter, and enchiladas in green or red chili sauce are among the tasty offerings. ✉ *Hidalgo 2,* ☎ *762/2–11–70. Reservations not accepted. AE, MC, V.*

$ ✕ **Señor Costilla.** That's right. This translates as Mr. Ribs, and the whimsical name says it all. The Taxco outpost of the zany Anderson chain serves barbecued ribs and chops in a restaurant with great balcony seating. ✉ *Plaza Borda 1,* ☎ *762/2–32–15. Reservations not accepted. MC, V.*

$$ **Hacienda del Solar.** This small resort (off Highway 95 south of town) was once the best in town. The rooms, grounds, and restaurant are still beautiful, but the surrounding neighborhood has seen better days. Its restaurant, La Ventana de Taxco (☞ *above*), maintains many loyal patrons. ✉ *Box 96, 40200,* ☎ *762/2–03–23,* FAX *762/2–03–23. 22 rooms with bath. Restaurant, pool, tennis court. MC, V.*

$$ **Monte Taxco.** A colonial style predominates at this hotel, which has a knockout view, a funicular, three restaurants, a disco, and nightly entertainment. ✉ *Box 84, Lomas de Taxco, 40200,* ☎ *762/2–13–00,* FAX *762/2–14–28. 156 rooms, suites, and villas with bath. 3 restaurants, 9-hole golf course, 3 tennis courts, horseback riding, dance club. AE, DC, MC, V.*

$$ ★ **Posada de la Misión.** Laid out like a village, this hotel is close to town. The pool area is adorned with murals by the noted Mexican artist Juan O'Gorman. ✉ *Box 88, Cerro de la Misión 32, 40230,* ☎ *762/2–00–63,* FAX *762/2–21–98. 150 rooms with bath. Pool. AE, DC, MC, V.*

$ **Agua Escondida.** Popular with some regular visitors to Taxco, this small hotel has simple rooms decorated with Mexican-style furnishings. ✉ *Guillermo Spratling 4, 40200,* ☎ *762/2–07–26,* FAX *762/2–13–06. 50 rooms with bath. Restaurant, café-bar, pool. MC, V.*

$ **De la Borda.** Long a Taxco favorite, De la Borda is a bit worn, but the rooms are large and comfortable and the staff couldn't be more hospitable. Ask for a room overlooking town. There's a restaurant with occasional entertainment, and many bus tours en route from Mexico City to Acapulco stay here overnight. ⊠ *Box 6, Cerro del Pedregal 2, 40200,* ☎ *762/2–00–25,* ℻ *762/2–06–17. 95 rooms with bath. Restaurant, pool. AE, MC, V.*

$ 🏨 **Los Arcos.** For those seeking lodgings in central Taxco, Los Arcos offers basic accommodations around a pleasant patio. ⊠ *Calle Juan Ruíz de Alarcón 12, 40200,* ☎ *762/2–18–36,* ℻ *762/2–32–11. 25 rooms with bath. MC, V.*

$ 🏨 **Posada de los Castillo.** This in-town inn is straightforward, clean, and good for the price. The Emilia Castillo silver shop is off the lobby. ⊠ *Juan Ruíz de Alarcón 7, 40200,* ☎ *762/2–13–96,* ℻ *762/2–34–71. 15 rooms with bath. DC, MC, V.*

$ 🏨 **Posada de San Javier.** This sprawling, very private es-
★ tablishment is set somewhat haphazardly around a charming garden with a pool and wishing well. In addition to the rooms, there are seven one-bedroom apartments with living rooms and kitchenettes (generally monopolized by wholesale silver buyers). ⊠ *Estacas 1 or Exrastro 4, 40200,* ☎ *762/2–31–77,* ℻ *762/2–00–80. 25 rooms with bath. MC, V.*

$ 🏨 **Rancho Taxco-Victoria.** This in-town hotel, in two buildings connected by a bridge over the road, is under the same management as the De la Borda (☞ *above*). Like the De la Borda, it is past its prime but exudes a certain charm. The rooms have been freshly painted, and the Mexican decor is simple but attractive. There's also the requisite splendid view. ⊠ *Box 83, Carlos J. Nibbi 5, 40200,* ☎ *762/2–02–10,* ℻ *762/2–00–10. 64 rooms with bath. Restaurant, bar, pool. AE, MC, V.*

$ 🏨 **Santa Prisca.** The patio with fountains is a plus at this colonial-style hotel. ⊠ *Cena Obscuras 1, 40200,* ☎ ℻ *762/2–00–80. 40 rooms. Restaurant, bar. AE, MC, V.*

Nightlife and the Arts

FESTIVALS

Except for the Jornadas Alarconas—which honors one of Mexico's greatest dramatists with theater, dance and concerts (dates change every year)—Taxco has no abundance of cultural events. But it *is* noted for its festivals, an integral part of the town's character. These fiestas provide an opportunity to honor almost every saint in heaven with music, dancing, marvelous fireworks (Taxco is Mexico's fireworks capital), and lots of fun. The people of Taxco demonstrate their pyrotechnical skills with set pieces—wondrous blazing "castles" made of bamboo. (Note: Expect high occupancy at local hotels and inns during fiestas.)

January 18, the feast of Santa Prisca and San Sebastián, the town's patron saints, is celebrated with music and fireworks.

Holy Week, from Palm Sunday to Easter Sunday, brings processions and events that blend Christian and Indian traditions; the dramas involve hundreds of participants, images of Christ, and, for one particular procession, black-hooded penitents. Most events are centered on Plaza Borda and the Santa Prisca Church.

September 29, Saint Michael's Day (Dia de San Miguel), is celebrated with regional dances and pilgrimages to the Chapel of Saint Michael the Archangel.

In **early November,** on the Monday following the Day of the Dead celebrations on November 1 and 2, the entire town takes off to a nearby hill for the Fiesta de los Jumiles. The *jumil* is a crawling insect that is said to taste strongly of iodine and is considered a great delicacy. Purists eat them alive, but others prefer them stewed, fried, or combined with chili in a hot sauce.

In **late November or early December,** the National Silver Fair (Feria Nacional de la Plata) draws hundreds of artisans from around the world for a variety of displays, concerts, exhibitions, and contests held around the city.

NIGHTLIFE

Travelers should satisfy their appetite for fun after dark in Acapulco. Taxco has a few discos (open only on weekends), a couple of piano bars, and some entertainment, but the range is limited.

Still, you might enjoy spending an evening perched on a chair on a balcony or in one of the cafés surrounding the Plaza Borda. Two traditional favorites are the **Bar Paco** (⊠ Plaza Borda 12, ☎ 762/2–00–63) and **Bertha's** (⊠ Plaza Borda

9, ☎ 762/2–01–72), where a tequila, lime, and club-soda concoction called a Bertha is the house specialty. In addition, some of the town's best restaurants have music on weekends.

Or immerse yourself in the thick of things, especially on Sunday evening, by settling in on a wrought-iron bench on the zócalo to watch children, lovers, and fellow people-watchers.

Most of Taxco's nighttime activity is at the Monte Taxco hotel, either at the **Bongolé** discotheque or at **Tony's Bar**, where the Papantla fliers ($6) perform nightly, except Sunday. On Saturday nights, the hotel offers a buffet, a terrific fireworks display, and a show put on by the hotel's employees.

Outdoor Activities and Sports

You can play golf or tennis, swim, and ride horses at a few hotels around Taxco. Call to see if the facilities are open to nonguests. Bullfights are occasionally held in the small town of Acmixtla, 6 kilometers (4 miles) from Taxco. Ask at your hotel about the schedule.

Shopping

Crafts

Lacquered gourds and boxes from the town of Olinalá, masks, bowls, straw baskets, bark paintings, and many other handcrafted items native to the state of Guerrero are available from strolling vendors and are displayed on the cobblestones at "sidewalk boutiques."

Arnoldo (⊠ Palma 1, ☎ 762/2–12–72) has an interesting collection of ceremonial masks; originals come with a certificate of authenticity as well as a written description of origin and use.

Elsa Ruíz de Figueroa (⊠ Plazuela de San Juan 13, ☎ 2–16–83) offers a selection of native-inspired clothing for women, and a wide and well-chosen selection of arts and handicrafts.

Sunday is market day, which means that artisans from surrounding villages descend on the town, as do visitors from

Mexico City. It can get crowded, but if you find a seat on a bench in Plaza Borda, you're set to watch the show and peruse the merchandise that will inevitably be brought to you.

Silver

Most of the people who visit Taxco come with silver in mind. Many of the more than 1,000 silver shops carry almost identical merchandise, although a few are noted for their creativity. Three types are available: sterling, which is always stamped .925 (925 parts in 1,000) and is the most expensive (and desirable); plated silver; and the inexpensive *alpaca,* which is also known as German silver or nickel silver. Sterling pieces are usually priced by weight according to world silver prices; of course, fine workmanship will add to the cost. Work is also done with semiprecious stones; you'll find garnets, topazes, amethysts, and opals.

Bangles start at $3 and bracelets range from $10 to $250. Miguel Pineda, Tane and Los Castillo are some of the more famous design names. Designs range from traditional bulky necklaces (often inlaid with turquoise) to streamlined bangles and chunky earrings.

Alvaro Cuevas (⊠ Plaza Borda 1, ☎ 762/2–18–78) has fine workmanship to match its fine designs.

Emilia Castillo (⊠ Juan Ruíz de Alarcón 7, ☎ 762/2–34–71) is the most famous and decidedly one of the most exciting silver shops; it's known for innovative design and for combining silver with porcelain and other metals such as copper and brass. The artisans are disciples of Spratling.

The stunning pieces at **Galería de Arte en Plata Andrés** (⊠ Av. John F. Kennedy 28, ☎ 762/2–37–78) are created by the talented Andrés Mejía.

Joyería San Agustín (⊠ Cuauhtemoc 4, ☎ 762/2–34–16) carries a large collection of well-crafted silver jewelery and serving pieces. There's a branch at Talleres de los Ballesteros (⊠ Florida 14, ☎ 762/2–10–76).

Spratling Ranch (⊠ south of town on Highway 95, ☎ 62/2–61–08) is where the heirs of William Spratling turn out designs using his original molds.

Taxco A to Z

Arriving and Departing

BY BUS

First-class **Estrella de Oro** buses leave Acapulco several times a day from the Terminal Central de Autobuses de Primera Clase (⊠ Av. Cuauhtémoc 158, ☎ 74/85–87–05). The cost for the approximately 5½-hour ride is about $10 one way for deluxe service. The Taxco terminal is at Avenida John F. Kennedy 126 (☎ 762/2–06–48). First-class **Flecha Roja** buses depart Acapulco several times a day from the Terminal de Autobuses (⊠ Ejido 47, ☎ 74/69–20–29). The one-way ticket is about $8 for first-class service. The Taxco terminal for this line is at Avenida John F. Kennedy 104 (☎ 762/2–01–31).

BY CAR

It takes about three hours to drive from Acapulco, using the new—and expensive—toll road. It is common practice to take an overnight tour. Check with your hotel for references and prices.

Transportation

Unless you're used to byways, alleys, and tiny streets, maneuvering anything bigger than your two feet through Taxco will be difficult. Fortunately, almost everything of interest is within walking distance of the zócalo. Minibuses travel along preset routes and charge only a few cents, and Volkswagen "bugs" provide inexpensive (average $1) taxi transportation. Remember that Taxco's altitude is 5,800 feet. Wear sensible shoes for negotiating the hilly streets, and if you have come from sea level, take it easy on your first day.

Visitor Information

Tourism Office: ⊠ Av. de los Plateros 1, ☎ 762/2–22–74. ☉ Weekdays 9–2 and 4–7.

IXTAPA AND ZIHUATANEJO

One of the most appealing of the Pacific Coast destinations, Ixtapa/Zihuatanejo offers visitors a taste of both Mexico present and past. Ixtapa (pronounced eeks-*tah*-pa), where most Americans stay—probably because they can't pronounce Zihuatanejo (see-wha-tah-*nay*-ho)—is young and glitzy. Exclusively a vacation resort, it was created in the early 1970s by Fonatur, Mexico's National Fund for Tourism Development, which also brought us Cancún. World-class hotels cluster in the Hotel Zone around Palmar Bay, where conditions are ideal for swimming and water sports; across the road are clusters of shopping plazas. The hotels are well spaced; there's always plenty of room on the beach, which is lighted for strolling at night; and the pace is leisurely.

Zihuatanejo, only 7 kilometers (4 miles) down the coast (southeast) from Ixtapa, is an old fishing village on a picturesque sheltered bay. Until the advent of Ixtapa, it was hardly known even among Mexicans. But long before Columbus sailed to America, Zihuatanejo was a sanctuary for indigenous nobility. Figurines, ceramics, stone carvings, and stelae still being found in the area verify the presence of civilizations dating as far back as the Olmecs (3000 BC). The original name, Cihuatlán, means "place of women" in the Náhuatl language. Weaving was likely the dominant industry in this matriarchal society, as evidenced by pre-Hispanic figurines, bobbins, and other related artifacts found in the area.

In 1527, Spanish conquistadors launched a trade route from Zihuatanejo Bay to the Orient. Galleons returned with silks, spices, and, according to some historians, the first coconut palms to arrive in America, brought from the Philippines. But the Spaniards did little colonizing here. A scout sent by Hernán Cortés reported back to the conquistador that the place was nothing great, tagging the name Cihuatlán with the demeaning Spanish suffix "nejo,"—hence "Zihuatanejo."

With the advent of Ixtapa, Zihuatanejo began to grow and the little dirt streets were paved with decorative brick. The place has managed to retain its charm, but it's also the area's municipal center, and its *malecón* (waterfront) and narrow streets are lined with hotels, restaurants, and boutiques.

Exploring Ixtapa and Zihuatanejo

Ixtapa and Zihuatenejo have few sights per se, but they're both pleasant places to stroll—the former especially if you enjoy a modern beach ambience and shops, the latter if you like local color.

A Good Tour

The entire **hotel zone** in **Ixtapa** extends along a 4-kilometer (2-mile) strip of wide sandy beach called Playa del Palmar, on the open Pacific. It's fun to walk along the beach to check out the various hotel scenes and water-sports activities. Alternatively, you can stroll the length of the zone on **Boulevard Ixtapa,** a landscaped and immaculate thoroughfare; a series of Mexican village–style shopping malls line the boulevard across the street from the hotels. At one end of the hotel zone (when you enter from Zihuatenejo) is the 18-hole Ixtapa Golf Club, while on the other (generally described as being "up the coast," but actually lying to the northwest) you'll come to the Marina Ixtapa development, which includes a 600-slip yacht marina, a promenade with restaurants and shops, and the new 18-hole Marina Golf Course. If you want to venture out of this compact resort area, take a taxi 15 minutes up the coast to **Playa Linda;** it's a 10-minute boat ride from here to **Ixtapa Island** (☞ Beaches, *below,* for both), where you can spend the day eating, sunning, and swimming.

Zihuatanejo flanks a charming enclosed bay with calm beaches. A simple way to tour the town is to take a taxi to the **municipal pier** (*muelle*) from which skiffs continually depart for the 10-minute ride to **Las Gatas** beach (☞ Beaches, *below*), accessible only by water. The sportsfishing boats depart from this pier, too, and it's the beginning of the **Paseo del Pescador** (Fisherman's Walk) or **malecón,** which runs along the municipal beach, the most picturesque part of town. The brick-paved seaside path, only a quarter of a mile long, is lined with small restaurants and overflowing shops; you'll pass a basketball court that doubles as the town square. The malecón ends at the **Museo Arqueológico** (✉ East end of Paseo del Pescador, ☎ 753/3–25–52), where close to a thousand pre-Hispanic pieces as well as murals and maps are on permanent display; it's open

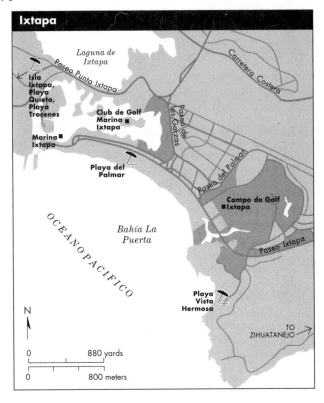

Ixtapa

Laguna de Ixtapa

Paseo Punta Ixtapa

Carretera Costera

Isla Ixtapa, Playa Quieta, Playa Trocenes

Club de Golf Marina Ixtapa ■

Paseo de las Garzas

Paseo del Palmar

Marina Ixtapa ■

Playa del Palmar

Campo de Golf ■**Ixtapa**

Bahía La Puerta

OCEANO PACIFICO

Paseo Ixtapa

Playa Vista Hermosa

N

TO ZIHUATANEJO →

| 0 | | 880 yards |
| 0 | | 800 meters |

Tuesday–Sunday 10–6. If you continue beyond the museum, you can take a footpath cut into the rocks to **Playa la Madera** (☞ Beaches, *below*).

Beaches

Ixtapa

IXTAPA ISLAND

The most popular beach on Ixtapa Island is **Playa Cuacha-lalate,** named for a local tree whose bark has been used as

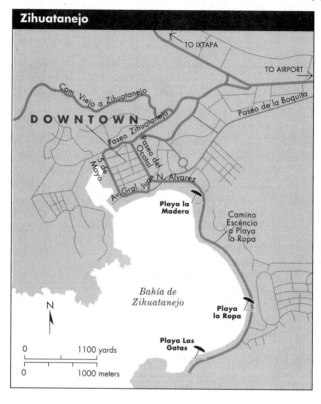

Zihuatanejo

TO IXTAPA

TO AIRPORT

Cam. Viejo a Zihuatanejo

Paseo de la Boquita

D O W N T O W N

Paseo Zihuatanejo

Paseo del Ocotal

5 de Mayo

Av. Gral. Juan N. Alvarez

Playa la Madera

Camino Escéncio a Playa la Ropa

Bahía de Zihuatanejo

N

Playa la Ropa

Playa Las Gatas

| 0 | 1100 yards |
| 0 | 1000 meters |

a remedy for kidney ailments since ancient times. This beach is lined with good seafood eateries. A short walk across to the other side of the island takes you to the gorgeous sandy **Varadero beach,** a wonderful spot for sunset viewing. It is also lined with small restaurants, and there are water-sports facilities. Just behind the restaurants is **Playa Coral,** with crystal-clear water that's ideal for snorkeling. **Playa Carey,** toward the south end of the island, is small and isolated. The pangas (motor-powered skiffs) run between the boat landings at both Cuachalalate and Varadero beaches and Playa Linda on the mainland.

PLAYA DEL PALMAR

Ixtapa's main beach, this 4-kilometer (2-mile)-long broad sandy stretch runs along the Hotel Zone. Water-sports facilities are available all along the shore. Since this is essentially open sea, the surf can be quite strong.

PLAYA LINDA

About 10 minutes beyond the Ixtapa Hotel Zone, the long, pristine Playa Linda has a handicraft mart at its edge, as well as a rock jetty from which covered pangas take passengers on a 10-minute ride to Ixtapa Island (☞ *above*). The boats run continuously from early morning until 5 PM. A round-trip costs about $2 (hold on to your ticket stub for the return).

Zihuatanejo

PLAYA LA MADERA

Across Zihuatanejo Bay from Playa Principal, Playa la Madera may be reached via a seaside footpath cut into the rocks. Also accessible by car, this pancake-flat beach with calm water has a sprinkling of small hotels and restaurants. It was named madera or "wood" beach because it was a Spanish port for shipping oak, pine, cedar and mahogany cut from the nearby Sierra Madre Sur.

PLAYA LA ROPA

On the other side of a rocky point, Playa la Ropa is the most beautiful beach in the area; it's a five-minute taxi ride from town. Along this 1-kilometer (½-mile) stretch of soft sand are water-sports facilities, open-air restaurants, and a few hotels. It got its name ("clothes beach") when a Spanish galleon returning from the Orient ran aground here, strewing its cargo of silks and clothing.

PLAYA LAS GATAS

Named for the gatas (docile nurse sharks) that used to linger here, this beach has a mysterious long row of hewn rocks just offshore that serves as a breakwater. Legend has it that Tarascan King Calzontzin built it to shelter his royal daughter's private beach. It is now lined with simple seafood eateries that also have lounge chairs for sunning. There is

also good snorkeling here. Las Gatas is accessible only by
boat, and small pangas run continuously to and from the
municipal pier until 5 PM. Purchase your round-trip ticket
(about $2) at the Cooperativa office at the beginning of the
pier. Keep the ticket stub for your return trip.

PLAYA PRINCIPAL

At the edge of town, the town's picturesque main beach is
rimmed by the Paseo del Pescador (fisherman's walk). Here
local fishermen keep their skiffs and gear used for nightly
fishing journeys out to sea. They return here in the morning to sell their catch to the local townspeople and to
restaurateurs.

Dining

CATEGORY	COST*
$$$$	over $35
$$$	$25–$35
$$	$15–$25
$	under $15

per person, excluding drinks, service, and 10% sales tax

Ixtapa

$$$$ ✕ **Bogart's.** Play it again: The setting is strikingly Moroccan,
à la the film *Casablanca,* and anyone who's been to any of
the links in the Krystal hotel chain is familiar with this exotic (and expensive) eatery. A Moorish fountain and piano
music add to the movie-theme atmosphere. The largely
Continental menu includes Suprema Casablanca, breaded
chicken breasts stuffed with lobster. ⊠ *Hotel Krystal, Blvd.
Ixtapa,* ☎ *755/3–03–03. Reservations essential. AE, DC,
MC, V.*

$$$$ ✕ **Villa de la Selva.** The multilevel cliff-top terraces offer
romantic views of the sunset, the stars, and the night-lit surf
breaking on the rocks below. Excellent international dishes
including grilled steaks, seafood, and Mexican specialties.
⊠ *Beyond Westin Brisas Resort on Paseo la Roca,* ☎ *755/
3–03–62. AE, DC, MC, V. No lunch.*

$$$ ✕ **Beccofino.** Part of the promenade along Marina Ixtapa,
this restaurant offers excellent northern Italian cuisine in
a serene Mediterranean-style atmosphere. There's alfresco

seating on a canopied deck that sits on the water. ⊠ *Plaza Marina Ixtapa,* ☎ *755/3–17–70. AE, DC, MC, V.*

$$$ ✕ **El Galeón.** Seafood lovers and people-watchers like to settle in at Marina Ixtapa's nautical-decor bar and outdoor terrace; there's additional seating on a simulated galleon right on the water. The fresh tuna steak is outstanding, and upscale Mexican fare is also available. ⊠ *Plaza Marina Ixtapa,* ☎ *755/3–21–50. AE, DC, MC, V.*

$$ ✕ **El Infierno y la Gloria.** "Hell and Glory" is a very typical Mexican cantina-bar and restaurant, serving an array of typical dishes. The food is good and you'll enjoy looking at the walls, hand-painted with Mexican scenes and allegories. ⊠ *La Puerta Shopping Center,* ☎ *755/3–02–72. AE, DC, MC, V.*

$$ ✕ **El Marlin.** This a great place to settle in at tables or beach lounges for some lunch, swimming, and sun. Simple, wholesome and delicious seafood dishes including (naturally) marlin: Try it steamed with vegetables in aluminum foil. El Marlin closes at 5 PM, when the last boats leave for the mainland. ⊠ *Varadero Beach, Ixtapa Island, no phone. No credit cards.*

$$ ✕ **Señor Frog's.** You can tell this is part of the Anderson chain of zany restaurants by the entrance signs that read, "Sorry, we're open" and "Members and nonmembers only." As usual the atmosphere is raucous and the food—tapas, burgers, and Mexican dishes—plentiful and good. ⊠ *La Puerta Shopping Center,* ☎ *755/3–06–92. Reservations not accepted. AE, DC, MC, V. No lunch.*

$ ✕ **Marina Café.** Located at the base of the Lighthouse Tower on the Marina promenade, this upscale seaside stand serves everything from pizza to sushi, tacos, and cocktails. Seating is outdoors on plastic chairs. ⊠ *Marina Ixtapa,* ☎ *755/3–22–88. Reservations not accepted. No credit cards.*

$ ✕ **Nueva Zelanda.** From breakfast through dinner everybody drops in to this sparkling little coffee shop–style eatery which serves tortas (Mexican sandwiches on baguettes), and an array of fresh tropical fruit juices and fruit salads. ⊠ *Los Patios Shopping Center, behind bandstand, Ixtapa,* ☎ *755/3–08–38; Calle Cuauhtémoc 23, Zihuatanejo,* ☎ *755/4–23–40. Reservations not accepted. No credit cards.*

$ ✕ **Pizzeria Mamma Norma.** You can dine indoors or al-
fresco at this casual Italian eatery, which offers the best piz-
zas in town as well as wholesome salads. ⊠ *La Puerta
Shopping Center,* ☎ *755/3–02–74. Reservations not accepted. MC, V. No lunch.*

Zihuatanejo

$$$ ✕ **Kau-Kan.** Opened at the end of 1995, this restaurant
immediately became a local favorite. Owner-chef Ricardo
Rodriguez, previously the chef at the nearby Casa que
Canta and, before then, at Mexico City's Champs Elysées
restaurant, serves imaginative, exquisitely prepared seafood,
from fillet of sea bass to delicate manta ray in butter sauce.
Although the restaurant is right on Madera beach, the ser-
vice and setting are elegant. ⊠ *Playa Madera,* ☎ *755/4–
21–42. MC, V.*

$$ ✕ **Casa Elvira.** Opened in 1956, this Zihuatanejo institution has a pleasant dining room and serves a wide variety of
seafood and Mexican dishes. It gets crowded during high season. ⊠ *Paseo del Pescador 16,* ☎ *755/4–20–61. MC, V.*

$$ ✕ **El Patio.** Seafood and authentic Mexican dishes are
served in a delightful hacienda-style garden. There's live
music during high season. ⊠ *5 de Mayo 3,* ☎ *755/4–30–
19. AE, MC, V.*

$$ ✕ **La Perla.** Eat indoors if you want video sports bar action, or outdoors on La Ropa beach. Among the seafood
specialties, *filete de huachinango al vino blanco* (fillet of
red snapper in white wine) is a favorite. ⊠ *Playa la Ropa,*
☎ *755/4–27–00. MC, V.*

$$ ✕ **La Sirena Gorda.** Oil paintings and a bronze statue de-
pict the namesake "fat mermaid," and a small boutique sells
logo T-shirts and memorabilia. Specialties at this friendly
restaurant near the pier include seafood tacos and octopus
kebab. The setting is casual, with an outdoor patio. ⊠ *Paseo
del Pescador 20,* ☎ *755/4–26–87. Reservations not ac-
cepted. MC, V. Closed Wed.*

$$ ✕ **Paul's.** Swiss chef-owner Paul Karrer prepares every
entrée, including escargot, sashimi, duck breast, fresh quail,
and shrimp in dill sauce, with loving attention to detail. The
setting is far more casual than the menu. ⊠ *5 de Mayo across
from handicraft market,* ☎ *755/4–21–88. Reservations not
accepted. No credit cards.*

$$ ✕ **Rossy.** A local favorite for dining on the roof terrace or right on the beach. An array of seafood dishes includes a tempting shrimp-and-pineapple brochette. Musicians usually serenade diners on the weekends. ⊠ *South end of Playa la Ropa,* ☎ *755/4–40–04. Reservations not accepted. MC, V.*

$$ ✕ **Tamales y Atoles Any.** Jos Ramón González and his wife, Any, have created this Zihuatanejo favorite, famed for its authentic and wholesome Mexican fare. The vast menu includes moles, a wide selection of tamales, and green or white *pozole* (hominy stew), a Guerrero specialty—it's usually served only on Thursdays, but it's served daily here by popular demand. The fresh fruit drinks are excellent, too. ⊠ *Ejido and Vicente Guerrero,* ☎ *755/4–73–73. Reservations not accepted. AE, MC, V.*

$$ ✕ **Ziwok.** A play on the town's nickname, "Zihua," this small restaurant serves "wok-art" stir-fry dishes using fresh vegetables and seafood. ⊠ *Juan N. Alvarez behind La Sirena Gorda,* ☎ *755/4–31–36. MC, V. Closed Wed. No lunch.*

$ ✕ **Casa Puntarenas.** Talk about homey restaurants: Casa Puntarenas is not only family-owned and -operated, but it's also run out of the family residence. You'll select from a menu of seafood specialties and write your order on a piece of paper, which later becomes your check. To get here, cross the footbridge over the lagoon at the west end of the town near the pier (or take a taxi). ⊠ *Noria 12,* ☎ *755/4–21–09. Reservations not accepted. No credit cards. Closed in low season.*

$ ✕ **Garrobos.** Seafood specialties at this casual restaurant include *tiritas de pescado* (marinated strips of raw fish, typical of Zihuatanejo), and a house version of paella. Service is attentive. ⊠ *Juan N. Alvarez 52,* ☎ *755/4–29–77. Reservations not accepted. MC, V. No lunch.*

$ ✕ **La Mordida.** Join the throngs at this simple, very popular eatery for pizza and tasty charcoal-broiled burgers. ⊠ *Paseo de la Boquita 20,* ☎ *755/4–82–16. Reservations not accepted. No credit cards. No lunch.*

Dining and Lodging

Trocones

$$ ✕🖬 **El Burro Borracho.** For out-of-the-way seclusion, you can venture some 30 minutes northwest up the coast to the pristine 3-mile-long beach of Troncones, near the tiny village of the same name. Six comfortable stone cottages and a congenial restaurant-bar sit right on the beach. The menu ranges from cheeseburgers to fresh lobster; for breakfast, try the grilled pork chops with three eggs. Then lie in a hammock or go beachcombing, boogie boarding, hiking, or cave exploring. Owners Dewey and Carolyn are also known for their Casa de la Tortuga bed-and-breakfast, just up the beach. ☒ *Troncones Beach, Apdo. 277, Zihuatanejo, Guerrero 40880,* ☎ ꜰᴀx *755/4–32–96. 6 bungalows. Restaurant. No credit cards.*

Zihuatanejo

$$$$ ✕🖬 **La Casa Que Canta.** Resembling a thatch-roofed

★ pueblo village, "The House That Sings" is perched on a cliff side high above Zihuatanejo Bay. The multilevel palapa-topped lobby is adorned with folk art furnishings, including hand-painted chairs with Frida Kahlo motifs. The individually designed rooms, named for Mexican songs, also feature beautiful handcrafted pieces, and offer modern amenities such as air-conditioning and hair dryers. Because of the stepped architecture, the main swimming pool seems to be airborne. Below, overlooking the sea, a saltwater pool features a therapeutic whirlpool. Seven extra-spacious suites—five of them in a wing completed in early 1996—have their own pools. The multilevel restaurant offers fine Continental and Mexican fare as well as stupendous views (reservations required). Children under 16 are not accepted at either the restaurant or the hotel. ☒ *Camino Escénico a Playa La Ropa, 40880,* ☎ *755/4–27–22 or 800/525–4800,* ꜰᴀx *755/4–20–06. 23 suites. Restaurant, 2 pools, exercise room. AE, DC, MC, V.*

$$$$ ✕🖬 **Villa del Sol.** This is the ultimate in luxurious beach

★ living. One- and two-story suites in a series of casitas nestle amid coconut palms, lush tropical gardens, fountains, and meandering paths leading to Playa la Ropa, one of the loveliest beaches on the Pacific Coast. Guest rooms and baths are artistically designed, with canopied king-size beds, colorful folk art furnishings, and terraces or balconies with hammocks; all offer air-conditioning, satellite TV, minibars, and hair dryers, and some boast private outdoor hot tubs. You can sit under a palapa on the beach and order snacks, lunch, or drinks from a casual menu. In the evening, the European and Mexican chefs prepare fine international and local dishes, using the freshest of ingredients. Even if you're not staying here, don't miss the elaborate "Mexican Fiesta" buffet on Friday nights. Children under 14 are not accepted during high season. ⊠ *Playa La Ropa, Box 84, 40880, ☎ 755/4–22–39 or 800/223–6510, FAX 755/4–40–66. 36 1- and 2-bedroom suites. Restaurant, 2 pools, 2 tennis courts, beach. AE, DC, MC, V.*

Lodging

There is a wide range of hotel accommodations in Ixtapa and in Zihuatanejo. High-priced Ixtapa has almost exclusively deluxe, beachfront properties, and almost all are located along the Zona Hoteleria, a 4-kilometer (2-mile) stretch of Palmar Beach; they do not always match the other members of international chains whose names they bear in quality, however. Most of the budget accommodations are in Zihuatanejo, where the best hotels are on or overlooking La Madera or La Ropa beach and the least expensive are downtown. Two of the most exclusive small hotels in Mexico are in Zihuatanejo.

Most hotels raise their rates for the November–April high season; rates are lowest in the summer, during the rainy season. Price categories are based on high-season rates—expect to pay 25% less during the off-season.

CATEGORY	COST*
$$$$	over $160
$$$	$90–$160
$$	$40–$90
$	under $40

All prices are for a standard double room, excluding 10% tax.

JOB Representations (⊠ Villas del Pacifico Edifio C., Dept. 1, 40880 Zihuatanejo, Guerrero, ☎ FAX 755/4–43–74) specializes in apartment, home, and villa rentals.

Ixtapa

$$$$ 🏨 **Krystal Ixtapa.** This beachfront hotel, shaped like a boat with its bow pointing to the sea, is part of a Mexican chain. Rooms are standard contemporary style. The Club Krystalito provides recreational activities for children, and because of its meeting facitilities, the hotel is often filled with conventioneers. The Krystal is home to Christine, Ixtapa's most popular disco, and Bogart's (☞ Dining, *above*). ⊠ *Blvd. Ixtapa, 40880,* ☎ *755/3–03–33 or 800/231–9860,* 🅵🅰🆇 *755/3–02–16. 254 rooms and suites. 2 restaurants, coffee shop, pool, 2 tennis courts, dance club. AE, DC, MC, V.*

$$$$ 🏨 **Westin Brisas Resort, Ixtapa.** This immense, pyramid-
★ shape architectural wonder slopes down a hillside to its own secluded cove and beach, Playa Vista Hermosa. The grounds are luxuriant with jungle vegetation; fresh flowers on the bed welcome you to your room. Every vibrantly colorful unit has a private balcony with a hammock, ocean view, and a table for room-service dining; spacious junior suites offer larger balconies with hot tubs. Guests and nonguests enjoy the hotel's excellent Portofino and El Mexicano restaurants. ⊠ *Playa Vista Hermosa, Box 97, 40880,* ☎ *755/3–21–21 or 800/228–3000,* 🅵🅰🆇 *755/3–07–51. 428 rooms and suites. 3 restaurants, 2 bars, 3 pools, wading pool, 4 tennis courts. AE, DC, MC, V.*

$$$ 🏨 **Dorado Pacífico.** This privately owned beachfront hotel is known for its good service and fine food. The furnishings are fairly nondescript, but the ocean-view rooms have private balconies. Glass elevators look out on the dramatic atrium lobby and fountains. The hotel's recently installed health and fitness club is the most complete in Ixtapa. Try the beachside Cebolla Roja restaurant for lunch and dinner. ⊠ *Blvd. Ixtapa, 40880,* ☎ *755/3–20–25 or 800/448–8355,* 🅵🅰🆇 *755/3–01–26. 285 rooms and suites. 3 restaurants, bar, pool, 2 tennis courts. AE, DC, MC, V.*

$$$ 🏨 **DoubleTree.** Formerly the Omni, this beachfront hotel is located at the north end of the Hotel Zone, within easy walking distance of Marina Ixtapa. The Mexican colonial decor, with its bright pastel colors, is cheerful, and the new management has generally improved the place. La Gran Tapa Spanish-style restaurant features good paella and bullfight videos. ⊠ *Blvd. Ixtapa, 40880,* ☎ *755/3–00–03 or 800/222–8733, fax 755/3–15–55. 300 rooms and suites. 4 restaurants, 2 bars, pool, 2 tennis courts. AE, DC, MC, V.*

$$$ 🆄 **Presidente Forum Resort.** A member of the Intercontinental Hotel chain, this is the only all-inclusive property in the hotel zone: Room rates include all meals, beverages, and extensive recreational activities. If you want tranquility, request a room near the east pool, away from where the action is. ⊠ *Blvd. Ixtapa, 40880,* ☎ *755/3–00–18 or 800/327–0200,* 𝔽𝔸𝕏 *755/3–23–12. 400 rooms and suites. 3 restaurants, bar, 2 pools, wading pool, 2 tennis courts. AE, DC, MC, V.*

$$$ 🆄 **Villa del Lago.** This bed-and-breakfast in a modern colonial-style house is the only listed Ixtapa property that is not on the beach. It is, however, a golfer's dream, facing the 6th hole of the Campo de Golf Ixtapa (by Robert Trent Jones, Jr.). The two-level master suite, terrace, swimming pool offer views of the lush green course and the mountains beyond. Golf packages are available. ⊠ *Retorno Alondras 244, 40880,* ☎ *755/3–14–82; in the U.S., 619/575–1766;* 𝔽𝔸𝕏 *755/3–14–22. 6 suites. Library-lounge. AE, DC, MC, V.*

$$ 🆄 **Posada Real.** Smaller and more intimate than most of the other Ixtapa hotels, this member of the Best Western chain sits on Palmar Beach, has lots of charm, and offers good value. ⊠ *Blvd. Ixtapa, 40880,* ☎ *755/3–16–85 or 800/528–1234,* 𝔽𝔸𝕏 *755/3–18–05. 110 rooms. 3 restaurants, 2 bars, pool, wading pool, dance club. AE, DC, MC, V.*

Zihuatanejo

$$$$ 🆄 **Puerto Mío.** Just inside the mouth of Zihuatanejo Bay, this small hotel has a seaside level with a pool, terrace bar, dining room, guest rooms, and a marina where the Zihuatanejo Scuba Center is based. A hilltop "mansion" level features another pool and additional suites with sweeping bay views. Locals as well as guests enjoy the seafood, Continental cuisine, and romantic setting of the hotel's restaurant. ⊠ *Playa del Almacen, 40880,* ☎ *755/4–27–48,* 𝔽𝔸𝕏 *755/4–36–24. 31 rooms and suites. Restaurant, bar, 2 pools, yacht slips, scuba diving. AE, DC, MC, V.*

$$$ ☎ **Irma.** One of Zihuatanejo's originals, this simple and clean colonial-style hotel sits on a bluff overlooking Madera Beach (accessible by a stairway). ✉ *Playa la Madera, Box 4, 40880,* ☎ *755/4–21–05 or 800/336–5454,* ℻ *755/4–37–38. 73 rooms. Restaurant, bar, pool. AE, DC, MC, V.*

$$ ☎ **Avila.** In the center of town facing the beachside Paseo del Pescador, the Avila has large clean rooms (all are air-conditioned), TVs, and ceiling fans. ✉ *Calle Juan N. Alvarez 8, 40880,* ☎ *755/4–20–10,* ℻ *755/4–32–99. 27 rooms with bath. AE, MC, V.*

$$ ☎ **Bungalows Pacíficos.** Terraced down a cliff side above Madera Beach, each of the spacious bungalows has its own large veranda with a sweeping view of Zihuatanejo Bay as well as a fully equipped kitchen. The owner speaks Spanish, English, and German. ✉ *Cerro de la Madera, Box 12, 40880,* ☎ ℻ *755/4–21–12. 6 units. No credit cards.*

$$ ☎ **Catalina-Sotavento.** Really two hotels in one, this multilevel oldie-but-goodie sits on a cliff overlooking the bay. Below, accessible by extensive stairs, is Playa la Ropa and the hotel's beach bar and lounge chairs. Rooms are large and well maintained, with ceiling fans and ample terraces. ✉ *Playa La Ropa, Box 2, 40880,* ☎ *755/4–20–32,* ℻ *755/4–29–75. 120 units. 2 restaurants, 2 bars. AE, DC, MC, V.*

$$ ☎ **Las Urracas.** Each of the casita-style units has a porch in a shaded garden, a kitchen, and a stove. Located on La Ropa Beach, it is a great bargain—which lots of people know about, so reserve far in advance. ✉ *Playa La Ropa, Box 141, 40880,* ☎ *755/4–20–53. 16 bungalows. No credit cards.*

$$ ☎ **Villas Miramar.** This pleasant colonial-style hotel is in two sections (divided by a small street). The front section overlooks and has access to Madera Beach. Rooms, some with balconies, are nicely decorated and have tiled showers, air-conditioning, and ceiling fans. ✉ *Playa la Madera, Box 211, 40880,* ☎ *755/4–21–06,* ℻ *755/4–21–49. 17 rooms, 1 suite. Restaurant, bar. AE, MC, V.*

$ ☎ **Solimar Inn.** Near the town center, this comfortable hotel features large, air-conditioned rooms with kitchenettes, ceiling fans, and satellite TVs. Guests tend to stay for weeks or more. ✉ *Plazas los Faroles, 40880,* ☎ ℻ *755/4–36–92. 12 rooms. Bar, pool. MC, V.*

Outdoor Activities and Sports

Fishing

Ixtapa/Zihuatanejo is just being discovered as Mexico's new sportfishing destination. Anglers revel in the profusion of sailfish, black and blue marlin (the record is over 1,000 pounds), as well as yellowfin tuna and dorado. Aeromexico Vacations (☎ 800/245–8585), the airline's in-house tour program, offers comprehensive sportfishing packages including air, hotel, and sportfishing on specialized cruisers with expert bilingual skippers.

Bookings and information about sportsfishing can be obtained through **Ixtapa Sportfishing Charters** (✉ 33 Olde Mill Run, Stroudsburg, PA 18360, ☎ 717/424–8323, FAX 717/424–1016; in Zihuatanejo, ☎ 755/4–44–26 or 755/4–41–62).

Golf

There are two 18-hole championship courses in Ixtapa. The **Campo de Golf Ixtapa** (☎ 755/3–10–62), designed by Robert Trent Jones Jr., is on a wildlife preserve that runs from a coconut plantation to the beach. Part of the Marina Ixtapa complex, the highly challenging **Club de Golf Marina Ixtapa** (☎ 755/3–14–10) layout was designed by Robert von Hagge. Each has its own clubhouse with a restaurant as well as tennis courts. Green fees run approximately $55; caddies or carts cost about $20.

Horseback Riding

You can rent horses at Playa Linda just up the coast from Ixtapa, or at La Manzanillo Ranch, near Playa La Ropa in Zihuatanejo.

Scuba Diving

Some 30 dive sites in the area range from deep canyons to shallow reefs. The waters here are teeming with sea life and visibility is excellent. At the north end of Playa Cuachalalate on Ixtapa Island, **Nacho's Dive Shop** (no phone) provides rental equipment, instruction, and guided dives. The **Zihuatanejo Scuba Center** (✉ Calle Cuauhtémoc 3, ☎ FAX 755/4–21–47; also at marina of Hotel Puerto Mío), owned and operated by master diver and marine biologist Juan Barnard, offers one- and two-tank dives as well as an intensive five-day certification course. Divers can have their underwater adventures videotaped for an additional fee. This authorized NAUI (National Association of Underwater Instructors) Pro Facility has an enthusiastic and knowledgeable staff, including some expatriate Americans.

Tennis

All major Ixtapa hotels have night-lit tennis courts as do the **Campo de Golf Ixtapa** (☎ 755/3−10−62) and the **Club de Golf Marina Ixtapa** (☎ 755/3−14−10).

Water Sports

You'll find a variety of water sports along Playa del Palmar in Ixtapa. Parasailing costs about $20 for about a 10-minute ride; waterskiing and wave runners run about $30 per half hour; banana boat rides are about $5 for a 20-minute trip. On La Ropa beach, in front of Hotel Villa del Sol, Hobie Cats rent for $20 per hour and classes cost $30 per half hour. Windsurfers rent for $10 per hour; classes which include six hours over four days cost $40.

Nightlife

A good way to start an evening is a happy hour at one of Ixtapa's hotels. Sunset is an important daily event and plans should be made accordingly. Tops for sunset viewing (with live music) is the lobby bar at the **Westin Brisas Resort.** To follow sunset viewing by dancing to tropical music until about 2 AM, take the elevator up to the **Faro Bar** nightclub atop the 85-foot-high faux-lighthouse tower in Marina Ixtapa (☎ 755/3−20−90). **Christine,** at the Krystal in Ixtapa, is the town's liveliest high-tech disco, and a spectacular runner-up is **Euforia** alongside the Posada Real Hotel. **Carlos 'n' Charlie's** (✉ Blvd. Ixtapa, next to the Hotel Camino Real, ☎ 755/3−10−85) has a party atmosphere, with late-night dancing on a raised platform by the beach.

A number of hotels feature **Mexican Fiesta Nights** with a buffet, handicraft bazaars, and live folkloric music and dance performances. At the Sheraton, these take place every Wednesday, year-around. During high season, you'll find Fiesta Nights on Mondays at the Krystal and on Tuesdays at the Dorado Pacifico.

Shopping

Ixtapa

As you enter Ixtapa from the airport or from Zihuatanejo, you'll see a large handicrafts market, **Mercado de Artesanía Turístico** on the right side of Boulevard Ixtapa. The result of a state law that banned vendors from the beach, this market hosts some 150 stands selling handicrafts, T-shirts, folk apparel, and souvenirs.

Farther down on the right, across the street from the Hotel Zone, the shopping area is loosely divided into *centros comerciales,* or malls. These clusters of pleasant colonial-style buildings feature patios containing boutiques, restaurants, cafés, and grocery minimarkets. The first one you'll come to is **Los Patios,** where **Tanga Boutique** (☎ 755/3–05–98) offers a nice selection of Mexican and imported beachwear, and **La Fuente** (☎ 755/3–17–33) sells native-designed clothes, art, crafts, and home furnishings. Behind Los Patios, in a terra-cotta-colored building, is **Plaza Ix-pamar,** host to **El Amanecer** (☎ 755/3–19–02) and its nice array of folk art. Then comes **Las Fuentes,** where you'll find **Polo Ralph Lauren** (☎ 755/3–12–72); **Bye-Bye** (☎ 755/3–09–79) beach and casual wear; the ubiquitous sportswear emporium **Aca Joe** (☎ 755/3–03–02); and the handy **Supermercado Scruples** (☎ 755/3–21–28). The last mall on this strip is **La Puerta,** which includes **Ferrioni Collection** (☎ 755/3–23–43) with colorful Scottish terrier–logo casual wear, and **Mic-Mac** (☎ 755/3–22–66) for crafts and Mexican regional art and clothing.

Zihuatanejo

Downtown Zihuatanejo has a colorful **municipal market** with a labyrinth of small stands on the east side of the town center, on Calle Benito Juárez at Antonio Nava. On the west edge of town, along Calle 5 de Mayo, is the **Mercado de Artesanía Turístico,** similar to the craft and souvenir market in Ixtapa, but larger, with 255 stands. Good purchases include local hand-painted Guerrero wooden masks and ceramics, huaraches, and silver jewelry.

Near the mercado, across from the Aeromexico office and facing the waterfront, **Casa Marina** (✉ Paseo del Pescador 9, ☎ 755/4–23–73) is a two-story building containing several boutiques, all belonging to the same family. **El Embarcadero** has an extensive selection of folk art from all over Mexico; **Manos** sells handicrafts; **La Zapoteca** features hammocks and hand-loomed rugs; and **El Jumil** has an array of Guerrero ceremonial masks. You might want to poke around here first to check prices, and then head for the market, where you'll often pay less for the same wares if you have a good eye and are willing to bargain.

There are a number of interesting shops in the tiny three-block nucleus of central Zihuatanejo. **Galería Maya** (⊠ Calle Nicolás Bravo 31, ☎ 755/4–46–06) is very browsable for its folk art and leather goods. **Nando's** (⊠ Juan N. Alvarez 5, ☎ 755/4–22–38) features a selection of colorful hand-made tropical-chic women's apparel from Oaxaca and Chiapas. **Alberto's** (⊠ Calle Cuauhtémoc 12 and 15, ☎ 755/4–21–61) is one of the best places to find authentic Taxco silver jewelry. **Coco Cabaña** (⊠ Agustín Ramírez 1, ☎ 755/4–25–18) is a fascinating folk-art shop. Over at Playa Ropa, **Gala Art** (⊠ Hotel Villa del Sol, ☎ 755/4–22–39) exhibits and sells paintings and sculptures by prominent local artists.

Ixtapa and Zihuatanejo A to Z

Arriving and Departing

BY AIR

Ixtapa/Zihuatanejo International Airport is 9 miles from Zihuatanejo, 13 miles from Ixtapa. **Mexicana** (☎ 755/4–22–27) offers direct daily flights from Los Angeles and Chicago, while **Aeromexico** (☎ 755/4–22–37) flies direct every day from New York/JFK, Houston, Miami, and Dallas/Ft. Worth. Both airlines operate several daily nonstops (35 minutes) between Mexico City and Zihuatanejo. **Continental** (☎ 755/4–25–79) flies nonstop from Houston. Seasonally, **TWA** (☎ 755/4–52–20) has service from its St. Louis hub and **Northwest** (☎ 91–800/9–07–47) departs from Minneapolis/St. Paul.

BY BUS

Estrella Blanca (☎ 755/4–34–77) and **Estrella de Oro** (☎ 755–4–21–75) offer deluxe service (with air-conditioning, video, bathrooms, and soft drinks) between Acapulco and

Zihuatanejo. The trip takes less than four hours and costs about $15.

BY CAR

The trip from Acapulco is a 3½-hour drive over a good two-lane road that passes through small towns and coconut groves and has some spectacular ocean views for the last third of the way.

Contacts and Resources

CAR RENTALS

Hertz, National, and **Dollar** have locations at the airport and in Ixtapa and/or Zihuatanejo. A good local agency is **Quick Rent-A-Car** (⌧ Westin Brisas Resort, Ixtapa, ☏ 755/3–18–30).

EMERGENCIES

Police (☏ 755/4–38–37), **Public Safety** (Seguridad Publica) (☏ 755/4–71–71), **Red Cross** (☏ 755/4–20–09).

GUIDED TOURS

Most major hotels have lobby tour desks or travel agencies which offer a selection of sightseeing tours of Ixtapa, Zihuatanejo, and surrounding areas. Another option is a six-hour cruise on the 12-passenger trimaran *Tri-Star,* which sets sail from the Puerto Mío hotel marina in Zihuatanejo. For $60, you'll get an open bar (domestic drinks), live music, dancing, and a fresh-fish lunch at Ixtapa Island. You can also book a two-hour sunset cruise of Zihuatanejo Bay or a four-hour cruise to Playa Manzanillo, just outside the mouth of the Bay, for great snorkeling and swimming. For details about all of these cruises, contact **Yates del Sol** ☏ 755/4–35–89).

TRANSPORTATION

Unless you plan to travel great distances or visit remote beaches, taxis and buses are by far the best way to get around. Taxis are plentiful, clean, and reliable, and fares are reasonable and fixed. The fare from the Ixtapa Hotel Zone to Zihuatanejo is under $4. Taxis are usually lined up in front hotels. Two radio taxi companies are **APAAZ** (☏ 755/4–36–80) and **UTAAZ** (☏ 755/4–33–11). Minibuses run frequently between the Ixtapa hotels and between the Ixtapa Hotel Zone and downtown Zihuatanejo; fare is about 30¢.

Rental cars, from Jeeps to sedans with automatic transmission and air-conditioning, are available from major car-rental agencies (☞ *above*). You can also rent an electric-powered golf cart in Ixtapa from **Tropical Transportation** (⌧ Las Fuentes Shopping Center, ☎ 755/3–24–88). They're for local transportation only, however—don't consider taking one to Zihuatanejo—and cost from about $12 for one hour to $55 for 24 hours.

TRAVEL AGENCY

American Express (⌧ arcade of Krystal Hotel, Ixtapa, ☎ 755/3–08–53, ℻ 755/3–12–06).

VISITOR INFORMATION

Municipal Tourism Office (⌧ Zihuatanejo City Hall, ☎ 755/4–20–01), **Guerrero State Tourism Office** (⌧ La Puerta Shopping Center, Ixtapa, ☎ 755/3–19–68).

WHEN TO GO

The winter season (December through April) is when the Pacific Coast resorts are at their best, with temperatures generally in the 70s and 80s. The off-season brings humidity and mosquitos along with temperatures in the 80s and 90s, but at this time of year you'll also enjoy emptier beaches, warmer water (well into the 70s), and less crowded streets—as well as a 25% to 35% reduction in room rates and the opportunity to do a little bargaining on rental-car costs. Toward the end of the rainy season (June through September), which generally involves only brief daily showers, the countryside and the mountainous backdrop of the Sierra Madre del Sur turn brilliantly green with multicolored blossoms of trees and flowers.

10 Portraits of Acapulco

It helps to be pushy in airports.

Introducing the revolutionary new TransPorter™ from American Tourister. It's the first suitcase you can push around without a fight. TransPorter's™ exclusive four-wheel design lets you push it in front of you with almost no effort–the wheels take the weight. Or pull it on two wheels if you choose. You can even stack on other bags and use it like a luggage cart.

Stable 4-wheel design.

TransPorter™ is designed like a dresser, with built-in shelves to organize your belongings. Or collapse the shelves and pack it like a traditional suitcase. Inside, there's a suiter feature to help keep suits and dresses from wrinkling. When push comes to shove, you can't beat a TransPorter.™ For more information on how you can be this pushy, call 1-800-542-1300.

Shelves collapse on command.

American Tourister

Making travel less primitive.

©1998 American Tourister

Your passport around the world.

- Worldwide access
- Operators who speak your language
- Monthly itemized billing

Calling Card

MCI

415 555 1234 2244
J . D . SMITH

Use your MCI Card® and these access numbers for an easy way to call when traveling worldwide.

American Samoa	633-2MCI (633-2624)
Antigua†	#2
(Available from public card phones only)	
Aruba✜	800-888-8
Argentina★†	001-800-333-1111
Bahamas(CC)†	1-800-888-8000
Barbados	1-800-888-8000
Belize	815 from pay phones
	557 from hotels
Bermuda✜†	1-800-888-8000
Bolivia♦	0-800-2222
Brazil(CC)†	000-8012
British Virgin Islands✜	1-800-888-8000
Cayman Islands†	1-800-888-8000
Chile(CC)†	
To call using CTC ■	800-207-300
To call using ENTEL ■	123-00316
Colombia(CC)♦†	980-16-0001
Costa Rica♦†	0800-012-2222
Dominica	1-800-888-8000
Dominican Republic(CC)	1-800-888-8000
Ecuador✜††	999-170
El Salvador♦	800-1767
Grenada✜	1-800-888-8000

Guatemala♦	189
Guyana	177
Haiti(CC)✜	001-800-444-1234
Honduras✜	122
Jamaica	1-800-888-8000
(From Special Hotels only)	873
Mexico▲†	95-800-674-7000
Netherlands Antilles(CC)✜†	
	001-800-950-1022
Nicaragua(CC)	166
(Outside of Managua, dial 02 first)	
Panama†	108
Military Bases	2810-108
Paraguay✜	008-11-800
Peru	170
Puerto Rico(CC)†	1-800-888-8000
St. Lucia✜	1-800-888-8000
Trinidad & Tobago✜	1-800-888-8000
Turks & Caicos✜	1-800-888-8000
Uruguay	00-412
U.S. Virgin Islands (CC)†	1-800-888-8000
Venezuela✜♦	800-1114-0

To sign up for the MCI Card, dial the access number of the country you are in and ask to speak with a customer service representative.

http://www.mci.com

HOST TO THE WORLD

THE STORY of Acapulco begins with a Romeo-and-Juliet-like myth of the Yope Indians, who had been driven to Acapulco from the north by the Nahuas, forerunners of the Aztecs. Acatl (his name means "reed"), firstborn son of the tribal chief, heard a voice telling him that in order to perpetuate his race, he should seek the love of Quiahuitl ("rain"), daughter of an enemy chieftain. But after the two fell in love, her father refused to allow the marriage. Grief-stricken, Acatl returned to his home in the foothills of the Sierra Madre above the Bay of Acapulco, intent on being devoured by the animals. But Acatl missed the sweet warbling of the *zenzontle* bird and returned to the bay to lie beneath the mesquite tree, where he wept so hard that his body dissolved into a puddle of mud, which spread across the coastal plain. From the mud sprang little reeds, yellowish green tinged with red: These were the sons of Acatl, bearing the colors of the mesquite and the zenzontle. Quiahuitl, in turn, was transformed into an immense cloud and floated toward the bay where, finding her lost love, she dissolved into tears. The teardrops fell on the reeds, and Quiahuitl was united forever

with Acatl. This is said to be the origin of the name of Acapulco, which means "in the place where the reeds were destroyed." The legend holds that whenever the bay is threatened by clouds, Quiahuitl, remembering her love, is returning.

Acapulco has been inhabited since at least 3000 BC; the oldest Nahua artifacts in the region date from 2,000 years ago. These artifacts—clay heads, known as the "Pretty Ladies of Acapulco"—were discovered in the lost city of La Sabana, in the hills outside Acapulco. Because of the earthquakes, the region contains few other archaeological remains.

From 1486 to 1502, after centuries under Tolec rule, Acapulco became part of the Aztec empire. It was then taken over by the Tarascans, another Indian tribe, along with the rest of the province of Zacatula. It was such power struggles among the Indians that eventually led to Acapuclo's conquest by the Spaniards under Hernán Cortés. Montezuma II, the Aztec emperor, told Cortés that more gold came from Zacatula than from anywhere else so that Cortés would conquer Montezuma's rivals, the Tarascans, and leave his realm alone.

Acapulco was discovered by Francisco Chico on December 13,

1521, and has been a magnet for seekers of wealth ever since. Chico had been sent by Cortés to find sites for ports, since Cortés was obsessed with locating a route to the Spice Islands. Acapulco has a great natural harbor, twice as deep as either San Francisco or New York, and so was a perfect choice. In accordance with a custom of Spanish explorers, Chico named the bay after the saint whose feast day coincided with the day of his landing: Santa Lucía. Cortés then built a mule path from Mexico City to Acapulco—his Spanish overlords forbade the use of Indians to transport cargo—and used the settlement to build ships for his explorations of the South Pacific. In 1532, the town officially became a domain of the Spanish crown, known as the *Ciudad de los Reyes,* or City of the Kings. Cortés went frequently to Acapulco, staying at Puerto Marqués Bay, which was name for him (Cortés was the marquis, or Marqués, of the Valley of Oaxaca).

By 1579, Acapulco was booming, and King Philip II decreed it the only official port for trade between America and Asia—primarily the Philippines, which had been discovered by Spaniards sailing from Acapulco. (In the Spanish spoken in the Philippines, *acapulco* is the name of a plant, the *Cassia alata,* introduced to the Philippines by traders from Mexico.) For centuries afterward, the port played a

crucial role in the history of the New World: In 1537, Cortés sent ships to Francisco Pizarro to help his conquest of Peru, and two years later he launched an expedition to discover the Seven Cities of Cíbola. Ships from Acapulco explored Cape Mendocino, California, in 1602.

BUT IT WAS the Manila galleons—the *naos de China*—that brought Acapulco its early fame. The first vessel, the *San Pablo,* sailed in 1565, and for the next 250 years the Spanish crown maintained a stranglehold on trade with the Orient. The naos carried the richest cargo of their day: silks, porcelain, cottons, rugs, jade, ivory, incense, spices, and slaves. When goods from the East reached Acapulco, they were then carried overland—a 20-day journey along the 6-foot-wide Road to Asia trail—to Veracruz on the Gulf of Mexico, where other ships then bore the cargo to Europe. On their return voyages to the East, the galleons transported silver from Mexico and Peru. The Spaniards limited the traffic to one arrival a year, usually at Christmas, and this event was heralded by the great Acapulco Fair of the Americas. Traders and merchants came from all over New Spain to buy the goods, and the malaria-ridden village, normally home to 4,000 people (mostly blacks and mulattoes), was suddenly host to 12,000. Thus from its early days, Acapulco became well versed in the arts of hospitality. Because accommodations were insufficient to lodge the flood of visitors, locals developed a lucrative business by renting out house, patios, corrals, and even doorways. They made fortunes as entertainers, quack doctors, porters, food vendors, and water carriers. Visitors amused themselves with bullfights, cockfights, and horse races. So much Peruvian gold and silver changed hands that the mules were literally laden with coins, and the Spanish crown was obliged to remint the precious metals and exploit the Mexican silver mines.

ALL THIS WEALTH had several unfortunate consequences for Acapulco and New Spain. One was that the monopolies enjoyed by the guilds of Acapulco and Veracruz kept prices high and the demand for locally produced goods low. Eventually the Spaniards allowed two overland journeys a year and established other ports to relieve the trade bottleneck.

The other outcome was the arrival of pirates. Until Sir Francis Drake's *Golden Hind* first sailed into Acapulco Bay in his exploration of the Pacific, the riches of

the Manila galleons were a Spanish secret. Drake, whose ship was shot at by panicking Spaniards, boarded their ship, stole the map to Manila, and a few days later intercepted one of the galleons. Drake informed Queen Elizabeth of his windfall, and from that day on, Acapulco was under constant siege by the likes of British pirates Thomas Cavendish, Henry Morgan, and William Dampier. (Treasure is still said to be buried off Roqueta Island.) The galleon crews arriving from Manila, exhausted from their journey and from malnutrition (food generally rotted during the long sea voyages), were never a match for the corsairs (English pirates), well fed from the excellent fishing in the Gulf of California. The first fort, the Castillo de San Diego, was built in 1616, and even it could not stave off the Dutch Prince of Nassau, who pillaged the city in 1624.

An earthquake destroyed the fort in 1776; its replacement, the Fuerte de San Diego, dates from 1783. In 1799, King Carlos IV declared Acapulco an official city, but shortly thereafter, its decline set in. With the independence movement in 1810, the fair was suspended; the arriving nao found the beaches deserted, and the captain was told to take his ship to San Blas. That same year insurgent leader José Maria Morelos attacked Acapulco, and a long and bloody siege ensued. The Acapulqueños, who were not particularly enthused by the prospect of losing the source of their livelihood, preferred continued allegiance with the Spanish empire to the dubitable gains of independence. Acapulco, an important source of revenue for Spain, was a natural target for the rebels, and Morelos burned it in 1814 to destroy its value.

Despite a devastating cholera outbreak in 1850, Acapulco enjoyed a brief revival in the 1850s, an outcome of the California gold rush. Ships stopped in Acapulco on their way to the Isthmus of Panama and returned to San Francisco carrying Mexican textiles. (Coincidentally, the great-grandson of "49er" John Sutter, Ricardo Morlet Sutter, was Acapulco's municipal president in the 1960s.) And in 1855 Benito Juárez, widely considered the father of modern Mexico, was sent to Acapulco to help bring down the dictator Antonio Santa Anna. A few years later, the city was bombarded by a French squadron during Juárez's fight against Emperor Maximilian, who had recognized Acapulco's strategic importance.

ACAPULCO resumed its fitful slumber through most of the 19th and early 20th centuries. An earthquake nearly razed the city in 1909; two years later it was invaded by some rebellious

lobos—Afro-Indians from the neighboring Costa Chica region descended from escaped slaves—who threw off the yoke of a tyrant, Johann Schmidt, during the early years of the Mexican Revolution. Modern Acapulco dates from the 1920s, when wealthy Mexicans—and adventurous gringos—began frequenting the somnolent village. With the opening of the first highway along Cortés's mule trail in 1928 and initial air service from the capital in 1929, Acapulco began to attract the Hollywood crowd and international statesmen. President Láaro Cárdenas (1934–40) started public works; the first telephone service began in 1936.

Ironically, it was Cárdenas's nationalism that modernized Mexico's hotel industry, thereby paving the way for the early foreign hotel entrepreneurs who would later dominate that sector of the economy. Cárdenas prohibited foreigners both from owning property within 50 kilometers of the Mexican coastline and from buying hotels. Foreigners circumvented the law either by becoming Mexican citizens or by setting up dummy corporations.

Thus it was a Texan, Albert B. Pullen, who first formed a company in the 1930s to develop the beautiful Peninsula de las Playas—now known as Old Acapulco—where many of Acapulco's first hotels rose. Pullen became a millionaire in the process, and a real-estate boom soon followed. J. Paul Getty was alleged to have purchased 900 acres of land at 3¢ an acre, some of which he used to build the Pierre Marqués ("Pierre" after his New York hotel of that name, "Marqués" after Cortés). In 1933, Carlos Barnard erected his first bungalows at El Mirador, atop the cliffs at La Quebrada, and other hotels followed suit.

But despite the growing tourist traffic, Acapulco still had the look, and appeal, of a humble town. Writers flocked to it: the reclusive B. Traven, author of *Treasure of the Sierra Madre,* ran a restaurant there from 1929 to 1947. Malcolm Lowry (*Under the Volcano*) first saw Mexico from his Acapulco-bound ship on November 2, 1936; that four-month sojourn was spent sampling the charms of tequila, pulque, mezcal, and Mexican beer. The playwright Sherwood Anderson visited Acapulco in 1938, and Tennessee Williams spent the summer of 1940 there. (Acapulco is, in fact, the setting for *The Night of the Iguana,* his celebrated play that John Huston later filmed in Puerto Vallarta.) That same year, Jane and Paul Bowles, the bohemian writer-couple, rented a house there, complete with avocado and lemon trees, a hammock, and their own tropical menagerie. At that time Acapulco boasted dirt roads, a wooden pier, no electricity, and a lot of mosquitoes.

WELL-HEELED foreigners first became interested in Acapulco during World War II, when most other pleasure spots were off-limits. In 1947, a two-lane highway improved accessibility, cutting travel time from Mexico City to a day and a half. By then there were 28,000 residents, compared to just 3,000 in 1931.

It was President Miguel Alemán Valdés (1946–52) who is credited with turning Acapulco into a tourist destination. Alemán ordered roads paved, streets laid out, water piped in, and public buildings erected. Even after his presidency, when he directed the newly formed National Tourism Council, Alemán was instrumental in the town's development. He was responsible for the new four-lane highway, which in 1955 made it possible to reach Acapulco from Mexico City in just six hours.

The jet-setters' invasion of Acapulco reached its peak in the 1940s and '50s. While many of them owned homes there, they still liked to congregate primarily at two hotels. Las Brisas was built in 1954 as a small cottage colony, Bermuda-style, by Juan March, on the former site of the fortress. The other watering hole was the Villa Vera Racquet Club. Originally a private residence for an Omaha businessman, it was later managed by Ernest Henri ("Teddy")

Stauffer, a Swiss swing bandleader who had fled the Nazis and settled in Acapulco, where he became affectionately known as "Mr. Acapulco." Stauffer also put up Acapulco's first discotheque, Tequila A Go-Go, and took over the popular La Perla restaurant at LaQuebrada, home to the cliff divers. The Villa Vera boasted one of Acapulco's many innovations, the first swim-up bar, and its first tennis club. (Another Acapulco first was parasailing.)

LANA TURNER used to frequent the Villa Vera's piano bar. Elizabeth Taylor married Mike Todd there, with Debbie Reynolds and Eddie Fisher as witnesses. JFK honeymooned in Acapulco, as did Brigitte Bardot and, many years later, Henry Kissinger. Yugoslav President Tito stayed there for 38 days, in one of 76 private homes owned by Las Brisas. President Eisenhower's visit in 1959 brought Acapulco even more publicity, as did an international film festival that debuted that year. Acapulco's guest list filled the society pages and gossip columns of America and Europe: Frank Sinatra, Johnny Weissmuller, New York Mayor Robert Wagner, Harry Belafonte, Douglas Fairbanks, Jr., Judy Garland, Sir Anthony Eden, John Wayne, Gina Lollobrigida, Gary Cooper, Edgar Bronfman, Jimmy Stewart, the Guinness family, Richard Widmark, Baron de Rothschild . . .

By the late 1950s and early '60s, Acapulco, which had also acquired the sobriquet "Nirvana by the Sea," was being called "Miami on the Pacific." It had long since ceased to be the exclusive haven for the rich and famous: Hotel construction had mushroomed, and the city's infrastructure could not keep pace with the growing resident population, then 100,000. La Laja, a seedy cluster of tenements outside town lacking sewers, drinking water, and electricity, swelled with 8,000 minimum-wage hotel workers known as *paracaidistas* (parachutists), or squatters. The government tried discreetly to squelch the city's social problems by selling the land at La Laja to the squatters, but also feared that move would encourage even more migration and aggravate unemployment. Hundreds of locals—mostly Indians from the surrounding region—were reduced to roaming the beaches, peddling kitschy folk art, tie-dyed beachwear, suntan oil, and soda.

By the mid-1960s, the government was eyeing the Port of Acapulco with renewed interest as a way to balance the economy and offset the seasonality of tourism. Acapulco was again trading, primarily with the Orient, and in 1963 some 180 freighters arrived, laden with Japanese appliances and automobiles. Each year, 60,000 tons of copra—dried coconut meat, used for making soap and margarine—left port; the copra industry was second to tourism in the region. The government wanted to capitalize on Acapulco's revived trade status by building a new port and opening a railroad to convey all the imports and locally produced copra, rubber, and wood pulp to Mexico City. But the projects never got off the ground.

SO TOURISM—which generated $50 million a year in direct spending—remained the key to Acapulco. With the advent of international jet travel in 1964, and the start-up of nonstop service from the United States in 1966, Acapulco's ascendancy became even more spectacular. The once lowly airport was dressed up in marble, and countless foreigners arrived to set up fashion boutiques and restaurants and indulge in the lucrative trade of marijuana and cocaine. Media stories continued to appear with great regularity, focusing largely on Merle Oberon Pagliai, the queen of Acapulco society, who spent six months a year in Acapulco in her Moorish-style villa, El Ghalal. Needless to say, that abode was as lavish as the nightly parties thrown about town by her fellow travelers, where socks were prohibited and themed events varied from disco nights (accompanied by the sounds of the Beach Boys) to costume frolics (all invitees dressed as Charles Addams's characters). *Coco locos*—a mouthful of coconut juice with a generous serving of rum, gin, or tequila, inevitably presented in a coconut shell—were all the rage.

But Acapulco's clients in the '60s—and today still—were not only the Beautiful People. The majority were actually Mexicans, to whom Acapulco was the equivalent of Atlantic City. In addition, there were vacationing college students—frequently indulging in midnight surf-dancing—seamen, and middle-class Americans who felt comfortable with the American-brand fast-food outlets lining the Costera Alemán, a south-of-the-border Coney Island.

Commercialization and unbridled growth took their toll on Acapulco in the 1970s. Belatedly, the government planned a $14 million project to pipe the city's sewage out to sea; prior to that the sewage had simply been carried in an open canal, and the hotels had installed their own services. Having reached the mature stage of its development, Acapulco found its glamour and popularity waning. That may have been a godsend for its 300,000 residents, crowded to the breaking point, as rural unrest in the surrounding countryside led increasingly to outbursts of violence. In the early 1970s, guerrillas assassinated Acapulco's police chief, kidnapped the state senator, and occasionally took hostages in Acapulco itself before most of the group was killed in gun battles.

As Acapulco waned, Mexico began looking elsewhere to practice its magic. In Iztapa, Cancún, Los Cabos, and now Huatulco, the government is attempting to avoid the mistakes it made in Acapulco through careful planning, while duplicating its formula of sea, sand, and sex. Several of those destinations now siphon off the tourism business. Whereas in the 1960s foreigners represented 45% of Acapulco's tourist revenue, by the mid-1980s that figure had slipped to 32%.

But Acapulqueños, who for centuries have derived their livelihood from commerce with foreigners, are intent on keeping their city afloat. In 1988, the public and private sectors banded together to refurbish the area known as Traditional (or Old) Acapulco, centered on Caleta Beach and the Zócalo. Hotels are being spruced up, street vendors are being paid to relocate to public markets, and the streets are undergoing a face-lift. And although one-third of Acapulco's one million residents still live in slums, that fact seldom intrudes on the tourist's conscience. In terms of sheer size, Acapulco is still the biggest of Mexico's tourist destinations. To many, it continues to epitomize the glamour and vitality for which it has long been celebrated. And though it will go through more permutations, Acapulco holds a secure place in Mexico's future.

— *Erica Meltzer*

A writer and trnaslator whose specialty is Mexico, Erica has been a frequent visitor there since 1967, and has lived in Mexico City.

THE CLIFF DIVE

JUST BEFORE THE DIVERS at La Quebrada in Acapulco take the long fall from the cliff into the surf, they kneel at a little shrine to Our Lady of Guadalupe and say their prayers. It's not hard to imagine what they ask her—I used to know the prayers they know—probably something like, "Remember, O most gracious Virgin, that never was it known that anyone who fled to thy protection, implored thy help or sought thy intercession was left unaided. Inspired by this confidence, I fly to thee, O Virgin of Virgins, my Mother. To thee I come, before thee I stand, sinful and sorrowful. O Mother of the word incarnate, despise not my petitions but in thy mercy hear and answer me: Let the water be deep enough, let the current be gentle, save me from garbage on the water, from the rocks, from blindness, from death, and may the *turistas* drop at least ten pesos apiece into the hat before they haul their fat white bodies back onto the buses."

I watched them dive half a dozen times one day. I sat on the terrace of the Mirador Hotel that overlooks the cliff with tequila and beer in front of me, telling myself I was trying to decide whether or not I would do this thing. I knew that the power of prayer wouldn't get me into the air off that rock. I've dived from heights before, but never that high, never out over rocks like those, never into a slash of water as narrow as that. Still, the only reason I was down there in the good tropical sun was to dive or to come up with an eloquent string of reasons why I hadn't. As it was, every time a Mexican dived, I was adding a because to my list of why nots.

One of them would walk out onto the rock and look down at the surf 130 feet below him. Then he'd kneel at the shrine, cross himself and pray. When he got up, he'd wander out of sight for a moment behind the little statue of Mary, then come back and stand for another five minutes on the edge while the tourists crowded the railings of the hotel terrace and filled the vantage points on the rocks below. Then he'd put both arms out straight in front of him, drop them to his sides, cock his legs, roll forward, and then spring with what looked like all his strength into a perfect flying arch. Foam boils up where the divers go in and the sound when they hit the water is like an old cannon going off. Then, a few seconds later, he'd be up, waving one arm and treading water against the white surge that was trying to slap him up onto the rocks.

AFTER a couple of divers and a couple of tequilas, I was telling myself I could live through it. I'd probably get hurt real bad, but it wouldn't kill me. I could get out past those rocks, all right, then it would just be a matter of going into the water as straight and skinny and strong as I could. I figured the worst I could get would be a broken back. Or else . . . or else I could sit right there on that terrace, have another shot of Cuervo, maybe six, lay back on my laurels and review the risks already taken. The worst I could get would be a hangover.

One of the divers came around to collect 50 cents. I gave him a dollar and when he said that was too much, I told him no, it wasn't. His name was Fidel and he had a broad face and a paunch that hung out over his tight red trunks. He looked about 40 years old. I asked him what kind of injuries the *clavadistas* got when they didn't hit the water right. Broken bones,

he told me, when the arms sometimes collapse into the head on impact. And the eyes, he said, if you break the water eyes first instead of with the top of your head, you go blind. But they have an association, he said, and the 26 divers in it have a fund, so that if one of them is hurt or killed, his family is taken care of. I didn't ask him if there was a fund for half-wit gringos with a history of foolish moments and a little too much sauce in them. There are no funds for people like that, people like me. Just simple services when the time comes.

Fidel moved off through the crowd, looking for more peso notes, and pretty much left me thinking there was no way in hell I was going to make that dive. The idea that I'd probably survive the plunge didn't mean nearly as much after he told be about the arms snapping over the head on entry. Somehow, I could *hear* that one. Even from 40 or 45 feet, which is the highest I've ever dived, you hit the water hard enough to make a moron out of yourself if you do it wrong. It *hurts* even when you do it right.

Finally, that afternoon, I figured out exactly what that cliff was to me. It wasn't a test of guts, or coordination, or strength, or Zen oneness with this imaginary existence. It was an intelligence test, the most fundamental kind of intelligence test: If you're intelligent, you don't *take* the test. Still, to sit there and think it through was one thing. I knew I had to let the animal make the final decision; take the meat up there onto that rock and let it look down the throat of this thing, let it *feel* the edge. There'd be no more maybes after that.

You actually have to climb down the rocks from the hotel to the spot from which they dive. On my way, I kept waiting for someone to stop me, tell me it was divers only out there, but no one did and there were no warning signs. I jumped a low stone wall and crept down some rock steps overhung with trees that made it feel like a tunnel out the end of which I could see the backside of the little shrine. It was cement, painted silver, and behind it, stacked like cordwood—as if to say that even among religious people liquor takes up where prayer leaves off—were two dozen empty tequila bottles. Two steps beyond that and I was out from under the green overhead and on the small flat pad from which they do it, and the scene opened before me: to my left, the hotel. I could see people tapping each other and pointing at me, as if to say, "Here goes another one, Edith." To my right, the flat blue Pacific stretched out to a sharp tropical horizon, and then turned into the sky. I stepped up and hung my toes over the edge, and then looked down at the rocks below me, then at the rocks on the other side, then at the skinny finger of water be-

tween them, rising and falling, foaming in and out. There were Styrofoam cups on the tide, pieces of cardboard and other trash I couldn't make out. I remembered my mother, who was a champion swimmer in the '30s, telling me about a woman high diver who'd gone off a 100-foot tower in Atlantic City and hit an orange peel on the water. She lived, but the image of their hauling her limp from the water has stayed with me, and it was never more vivid than at that moment at La Quebrada. Looking down from that cliff, your perspective is so hopelessly distorted it seems that, to miss the rocks on your side of the channel, you'd have to throw yourself onto the rocks on the other side. I tried to imagine myself through it. Get steady, feet together, arms down, roll, push, arch . . . but I couldn't take the fantasy any further than that. "No," I said out loud. "Just turn around and say goodbye to the Lady, Craig."

A couple of hours later, the defeat of the thing didn't seem very profound at all. If I'd kept drinking tequila, I just might have gone screaming off that cliff. Tequila, after all, talks to the animal in you and *he* thinks he can do anything when he's drunk.

After all, you gotta stop somewhere.

— *Craig Vetter*

Chicago is home for freelance writer Craig Vetter.

SPANISH VOCABULARY

Note: *Mexican Spanish differs from Castilian Spanish.*

Words and Phrases

Basics

English	Spanish	Pronunciation
Yes/no	Sí/no	see/no
Please	Por favor	pore fah-*vore*
May I?	¿Me permite?	may pair-*mee*-tay
Thank you (very much)	(Muchas) gracias	(*moo*-chas) grah-see-as
You're welcome	De nada	day *nah*-dah
Excuse me	Con permiso	con pair-*mee*-so
Pardon me/what did you say?	¿Como?/¡Mánde?	ko-mo/mahn-dey
Could you tell me?	¿Podría decirme?	po-*dree*-ah deh-*seer*-meh
I'm sorry	Lo siento	lo see-*en*-toe
Good morning!	¡Buenos días!	*bway*-nohs dee-ahs
Good afternoon!	¡Buenas tardes!	*bway*-nahs tar-dess
Good evening!	¡Buenas noches!	*bway*-nahs no-chess
Goodbye!	¡Adiós!/¡Hasta luego!	ah-dee-*ohss*/*ah*-stah -*lwe*-go
Mr./Mrs.	Señor/Señora	sen-yor/sen-*yore*-ah
Miss	Señorita	sen-yo-*ree*-tah
Pleased to meet you	Mucho gusto	*moo*-cho *goose*-to
How are you?	¿Cómo está usted?	ko-mo es-*tah* oo-*sted*
Very well, thank you.	Muy bien, gracias.	*moo*-ee bee-*en*, grah-see-as
And you?	¿Y usted?	ee oos-*ted*
Hello (on the telephone)	Bueno	*bwen*-oh

Numbers

1	un, uno	oon, *oo*-no
2	dos	dos
3	tres	trace
4	cuatro	*kwah*-tro
5	cinco	*sink*-oh
6	seis	sace
7	siete	see-*et*-ey

8	ocho	o-cho
9	nueve	new-ev-ay
10	diez	dee-es
11	once	own-sey
12	doce	doe-sey
13	trece	tray-sey
14	catorce	kah-tor-sey
15	quince	keen-sey
16	dieciséis	dee-es-ee-sace
17	diecisiete	dee-es-ee-see-et-ay
18	dieciocho	dee-es-ee-o-cho
19	diecinueve	dee-es-ee-new-ev-ay
20	veinte	bain-tay
21	veinte y uno/veintiuno	bain-te-oo-no
30	treinta	train-tah
32	treinta y dos	train-tay-dose
40	cuarenta	kwah-ren-tah
43	cuarenta y tres	kwah-ren-tay-trace
50	cincuenta	seen-kwen-tah
54	cincuenta y cuatro	seen-kwen-tay kwah-tro
60	sesenta	sess-en-tah
65	sesenta y cinco	sess-en-tay seen-ko
70	setenta	set-en-tah
76	setenta y seis	set-en-tay sace
80	ochenta	oh-chen-tah
87	ochenta y siete	oh-chen-tay see-yet-ay
90	noventa	no-ven-tah
98	noventa y ocho	no-ven-tah o-cho
100	cien	see-en
101	ciento uno	see-en-toe oo-no
200	doscientos	doe-see-en-tohss
500	quinientos	keen-yen-tohss
700	setecientos	set-eh-see-en-tohss
900	novecientos	no-veh-see-en-tohss
1,000	mil	meel
2,000	dos mil	dose meel
1,000,000	un millón	oon meel-yohn

Colors

black	negro	*neh*-grow
blue	azul	ah-*sool*
brown	café	kah-*feh*
green	verde	*vair*-day
pink	rosa	*ro*-sah
purple	morado	mo-*rah*-doe
orange	naranja	na-*rahn*-hah
red	rojo	*roe*-hoe
white	blanco	*blahn*-koh
yellow	amarillo	ah-mah-*ree*-yoh

Days of the Week

Sunday	domingo	doe-*meen*-goh
Monday	lunes	*loo*-ness
Tuesday	martes	*mahr*-tess
Wednesday	miércoles	me-*air*-koh-less
Thursday	jueves	who-ev-ess
Friday	viernes	vee-*air*-ness
Saturday	sábado	*sah*-bah-doe

Months

January	enero	eh-*neh*-ro
February	febrero	feh-*brair*-oh
March	marzo	*mahr*-so
April	abril	ah-*breel*
May	mayo	*my*-oh
June	junio	*hoo*-nee-oh
July	julio	*who*-lee-yoh
August	agosto	ah-*ghost*-toe
September	septiembre	sep-tee-*em*-breh
October	octubre	oak-*too*-breh
November	noviembre	no-vee-*em*-breh
December	diciembre	dee-see-*em*-breh

Useful Phrases

Do you speak English?	¿Habla usted inglés?	*ah*-blah oos-*ted* in-*glehs*
I don't speak Spanish	No hablo español	no *ah*-blow es-pahn-*yol*
I don't understand (you)	No entiendo	no en-tee-*en*-doe
I understand (you)	Entiendo	en-tee-*en*-doe
I don't know	No sé	no *say*

I am American/ British	Soy americano(a)/ inglés(a)	soy ah-meh-ree-kah-no(ah)/ in-glace(ah)
What's your name?	¿Cómo se llama usted?	koh-mo say yah-mah oos-ted
My name is . . .	Me llamo . . .	may yah-moh
What time is it?	¿Qué hora es?	keh o-rah es
It is one, two, three . . . o'clock.	Es la una; son las dos, tres	es la oo-nah/sone lahs dose, trace
Yes, please/No, thank you	Sí, por favor/No, gracias	see pore fah-vor/no grah-see-us
How?	¿Cómo?	koh-mo
When?	¿Cuándo?	kwahn-doe
This/Next week	Esta semana/ la semana que entra	es-tah seh-mah-nah/lah say-mah-nah keh en-trah
This/Next month	Este mes/el próximo mes	es-tay mehs/el proke-see-mo mehs
This/Next year	Este año/el año que viene vee-yen-ay	es-tay ahn-yo/el ahn-yo keh
Yesterday/today/ tomorrow	Ayer/hoy/mañana	ah-yair/oy/mahn-yah-nah
This morning/ afternoon	Esta mañana/tarde	es-tah mahn-yah-nah/tar-day
Tonight	Esta noche	es-tah no-cheh
What?	¿Qué?	keh
What is it?	¿Qué es esto?	keh es es-toe
Why?	¿Por qué?	pore keh
Who?	¿Quién?	kee-yen
Where is . . . ? the train station?	¿Dónde está . . . ? la estación del tren?	dohn-day es-tah la es-tah-see-on del train
the subway station?	la estación del Metro?	la es-ta-see-on del meh-tro
the bus stop?	la parada del autobús?	la pah-rah-dah del oh-toe-boos
the post office?	la oficina de correos?	la oh-fee-see-nah day koh-reh-os
the bank?	el banco?	el bahn-koh
the . . . hotel?	el hotel . . . ?	el oh-tel
the store?	la tienda . . . ?	la tee-en-dah
the cashier?	la caja?	la kah-hah
the . . . museum?	el museo . . . ?	el moo-seh-oh
the hospital?	el hospital?	el ohss-pea-tal
the elevator?	el ascensor?	el ah-sen-sore
the bathroom?	el baño?	el bahn-yoh

Here/there	Aquí/allá	ah-*key*/ah-*yah*
Open/closed	Abierto/cerrado	ah-be-*er*-toe/ ser-*ah*-doe
Left/right	Izquierda/derecha	iss-key-*er*-dah/ dare-*eh*-chah
Straight ahead	Derecho	der-*eh*-choh
Is it near/far?	¿Está cerca/lejos?	es-*tah* sair-kah/ *leh*-hoss
I'd like . . .	Quisiera . . .	kee-see-*air*-ah
a room	un cuarto/una habitación	oon *kwahr*-toe/ oo-nah ah-bee-tah-see-*on*
the key	la llave	lah *yah*-vay
a newspaper	un periódico	oon pear-ee-*oh*-dee-koh
a stamp	un timbre de correo	oon *team*-bray day koh-*reh*-oh
I'd like to buy . . .	Quisiera comprar . . .	kee-see-*air*-ah kohm-*prahr*
cigarettes	cigarrillo	ce-gar-*reel*-oh
matches	cerillos	ser-*ee*-ohs
a dictionary	un diccionario	oon deek-see-oh-*nah*-ree-oh
soap	jabón	hah-*bone*
a map	un mapa	oon *mah*-pah
a magazine	una revista	oon-ah reh-*veess*-tah
paper	papel	pah-*pel*
envelopes	sobres	so-brace
a postcard	una tarjeta postal	oon-ah tar-*het*-ah post-*ahl*
How much is it?	¿Cuánto cuesta?	*kwahn*-toe *kwes*-tah
It's expensive/ cheap	Está caro/barato	es-*tah* kah-roh/ bah-*rah*-toe
A little/a lot	Un poquito/ mucho . . .	oon poh-*kee*-toe/ *moo*-choh
More/less	Más/menos	mahss/*men*-ohss
Enough/too much/too little	Suficiente/de- masiado/muy poco	soo-fee-see-*en*-tay/ day-mah-see-*ah*-doe/*moo*-ee poh-koh
Telephone	Teléfono	tel-*ef*-oh-no
Telegram	Telegrama	teh-leh-*grah*-mah
I am ill/sick	Estoy enfermo(a)	es-*toy* en-*fair*-moh(ah)
Please call a doctor	Por favor llame un médico	pore fa-*vor* ya-may oon *med*-ee-koh
Help!	¡Auxilio! ¡Ayuda!	owk-*see*-lee-oh/ ah-*yoo*-dah

| Fire! | ¡Encendio! | en-*sen*-dee-oo |
| Caution!/Look out! | ¡Cuidado! | kwee-*dah*-doh |

On the Road

Highway	Carretera	car-ray-*ter*-ah
Causeway, paved highway	Calzada	cal-*za*-dah
Route	Ruta	*roo*-tah
Road	Camino	cah-*mee*-no
Street	Calle	*cah*-yeh
Avenue	Avenida	ah-ven-*ee*-dah
Broad, tree-lined boulevard	Paseo	pah-*seh*-oh
Waterfront promenade	Malecón	mal-lay-*cone*
Wharf	Embarcadero	em-bar-cah-*day*-ro

In Town

Church	Templo/Iglesia	*tem*-plo/e-*gles*-se-ah
Cathedral	Catedral	cah-tay-*dral*
Neighborhood	Barrio	*bar*-re-o
Foreign exchange shop	Casa de cambio	*cas*-sah day *cam*-be-o
City hall	Ayuntamiento	ah-yoon-tah-mee *en*-toe
Main square	Zócalo	*zo*-cal-o
Traffic circle	Glorieta	glor-e-*ay*-tah
Market	Mercado (Spanish)/ Tianguis (Indian)	mer-*cah*-doe/ tee-*an*-geese
Inn	Posada	pos-*sah*-dah
Group taxi	Colectivo	co-lec-*tee*-vo
Group taxi along fixed route	Pesero	pi-*seh*-ro

Items of Clothing

Embroidered white smock	Huipil	whee-*peel*
Pleated man's shirt worn outside the pants	Guayabera	gwah-ya-*beh*-ra
Leather sandals	Huaraches	wah-*ra*-chays
Shawl	Rebozo	ray-*bozh*-o
Pancho or blanket	Serape	seh-*ra*-peh

Dining Out

A bottle of . . .	Una botella de . . .	*oo*-nah bo-*tay*-yah deh
A cup of . . .	Una taza de . . .	*oo*-nah *tah*-sah deh
A glass of . . .	Un vaso de . . .	oon *vah*-so deh
Ashtray	Un cenicero	oon sen-ee-*seh*-roh
Bill/check	La cuenta	lah *kwen*-tah
Bread	El pan	el pahn
Breakfast	El desayuno	el day-sigh-*oon*-oh
Butter	La mantequilla	lah mahn-tay-*key*-yah
Cheers!	¡Salud!	sah-*lood*
Cocktail	Un aperitivo	oon ah-pair-ee-*tee*-voh
Dinner	La cena	lah *seh*-nah
Dish	Un plato	oon *plah*-toe
Dish of the day	El platillo de hoy	el plah-*tee*-yo day oy
Enjoy!	¡Buen provecho!	bwen pro-*veh*-cho
Fixed-price menu	La comida corrida	lah koh-*me*-dah co-*ree*-dah
Fork	El tenedor	el ten-eh-*door*
Is the tip included?	¿Está incluida la propina?	es-*tah* in-clue-*ee*-dah lah pro-*pea*-nah
Knife	El cuchillo	el koo-*chee*-yo
Lunch	La comida	lah koh-*me*-dah
Menu	La carta	lah *cart*-ah
Napkin	La servilleta	lah sair-vee-*yet*-uh
Pepper	La pimienta	lah pea-me-*en*-tah
Please give me	Por favor déme	pore fah-*vor* day-may
Salt	La sal	lah sahl
Spoon	Una cuchara	*oo*-nah koo-*chah*-rah
Sugar	El azúcar	el ah-*sue*-car
Waiter!/Waitress!	¡Por favor Señor/Señorita!	pore fah-*vor* sen-yor/sen-yor-*ee*-tah

INDEX

✕ = *restaurant,*   🏨 = *hotel*

NOTES

NOTES

NOTES

NOTES

NOTES

NOTES

Fodor's Travel Publications

Available at bookstores everywhere, or call 1–800–533–6478, 24 hours a day.

Gold Guides

U.S.

Alaska

Arizona

Boston

California

Cape Cod, Martha's Vineyard, Nantucket

The Carolinas & the Georgia Coast

Chicago

Colorado

Florida

Hawai'i

Las Vegas, Reno, Tahoe

Los Angeles

Maine, Vermont, New Hampshire

Maui & Lana'i

Miami & the Keys

New England

New Orleans

New York City

Pacific North Coast

Philadelphia & the Pennsylvania Dutch Country

The Rockies

San Diego

San Francisco

Santa Fe, Taos, Albuquerque

Seattle & Vancouver

The South

U.S. & British Virgin Islands

USA

Virginia & Maryland

Washington, D.C.

Foreign

Australia

Austria

The Bahamas

Belize & Guatemala

Bermuda

Canada

Cancún, Cozumel, Yucatán Peninsula

Caribbean

China

Costa Rica

Cuba

The Czech Republic & Slovakia

Eastern & Central Europe

Europe

Florence, Tuscany & Umbria

France

Germany

Great Britain

Greece

Hong Kong

India

Ireland

Israel

Italy

Japan

London

Madrid & Barcelona

Mexico

Montréal & Québec City

Moscow, St. Petersburg, Kiev

The Netherlands, Belgium & Luxembourg

New Zealand

Norway

Nova Scotia, New Brunswick, Prince Edward Island

Paris

Portugal

Provence & the Riviera

Scandinavia

Scotland

Singapore

South Africa

South America

Southeast Asia

Spain

Sweden

Switzerland

Thailand

Tokyo

Toronto

Turkey

Vienna & the Danube

Fodor's Special-Interest Guides

Caribbean Ports of Call

The Complete Guide to America's National Parks

Family Adventures

Fodor's Gay Guide to the USA

Halliday's New England Food Explorer

Halliday's New Orleans Food Explorer

Healthy Escapes

Kodak Guide to Shooting Great Travel Pictures

Net Travel

Nights to Imagine

Rock & Roll Traveler USA

Sunday in New York

Sunday in San Francisco

Walt Disney World for Adults

Walt Disney World, Universal Studios and Orlando

Where Should We Take the Kids? California

Where Should We Take the Kids? Northeast

Worldwide Cruises and Ports of Call

WHEREVER YOU TRAVEL, *H*ELP IS NEVER FAR AWAY.

From planning your trip to providing travel assistance along the way, American Express® Travel Service Offices are always there to help.

Acapulco

American Express Travel Service
Centro Comercial – La Gran Plaza
Costera Miguel Aleman 1628
Acapulco
74/691 133

Travel

http://www.americanexpress.com/travel

American Express Travel Service Offices are found in central locations throughout Mexico.